The
Princeton
Review®

ASAP
World
History

By the Staff of The Princeton Review

princetonreview.com

D1059733

Penguin
Random
House

The Princeton Review
110 East 42nd Street, 7th Floor
New York, NY 10017
Email: editorialsupport@review.com

Published in the United States by Penguin
Random House LLC, New York, and in Canada
by Random House of Canada, a division of
Penguin Random House Ltd., Toronto.

Terms of Service: The Princeton Review Online
Companion Tools ("Student Tools") for retail
books are available for only the two most recent
editions of that book. Student Tools may be
activated only twice per eligible book purchased
for two consecutive 12-month periods, for a
total of 24 months of access. Activation of
Student Tools more than twice per book is in
direct violation of these Terms of Service and
may result in discontinuation of access to
Student Tools Services.

ISBN: 978-1-5247-5768-7
eBook ISBN: 978-1-5247-5773-1
ISSN: 2575-4440

AP and Advanced Placement are registered
trademarks of the College Board, which is not
affiliated with The Princeton Review.

The Princeton Review is not affiliated with
Princeton University.

Editor: Colleen Day
Production Editors: Kathy Carter and
                   Otis Roffman
Production Artists: Deborah A. Silvestrini and
                   Craig Patches

Printed in the United States of America.

10 9 8 7 6 5 4 3 2 1

Editorial

Rob Franek, Editor-in-Chief
Casey Cornelius, VP Content Development
Mary Beth Garrick, Director of Production
Selena Coppock, Managing Editor
Meave Shelton, Senior Editor
Colleen Day, Editor
Sarah Litt, Editor
Aaron Riccio, Editor
Orion McBean, Associate Editor

Penguin Random House Publishing Team

Tom Russell, VP, Publisher
Alison Stoltzfus, Publishing Director
Jake Eldred, Associate Managing Editor
Ellen Reed, Production Manager
Suzanne Lee, Designer

Acknowledgments

The Princeton Review would like to thank the amazing content development team who built this book from the ground up: Kevin Kelly, Jean Hsu, and John Moscatiello. Thank you so much for your expertise, enthusiasm, brilliant ideas, and above-and-beyond dedication to this project.

We are also indebted to our outstanding production artists, Debbie Silvestrini and Craig Patches, for their stellar design, imagination, and endless patience and hard work. Thanks also to our production editors, Kathy G. Carter and Otis Roffman, for their time and attention to each page and detail.

Contents

Get More (Free) Content

1 Go to **PrincetonReview.com/cracking.**

2 Enter the following ISBN for your book: 9781524757687.

3 Answer a few simple questions to set up an exclusive Princeton Review account. (If you already have one, you can just log in.)

4 Click the "Student Tools" button, also found under "My Account" from the top toolbar. You're all set to access your bonus content!

Need to report a potential **content** issue?

Contact **EditorialSupport@review.com.**
Include:

- full title of the book
- ISBN number
- page number

Need to report a **technical** issue?

Contact **TPRStudentTech@review.com** and provide:

- your full name
- email address used to register the book
- full book title and ISBN
- computer OS (Mac/PC) and browser (Firefox, Safari, etc.)

The
Princeton
Review®

Once you've registered, you can...

- Get valuable advice about the college application process, including tips for writing a great essay and where to apply for financial aid

- If you're still choosing between colleges, use our searchable rankings of *The Best 382 Colleges* to find out more information about your dream school

- Access printable resources and bonus study material, including lists of the most important key terms, people, and ideas in world history

- Check to see if there have been any corrections or updates to this edition

- Get our take on any recent or pending updates to the AP World History Exam

Introduction

What Is This Book and When Should I Use It?

Welcome to *ASAP World History,* your quick-review study guide for the AP World History Exam written by the staff of The Princeton Review. This is a brand-new series custom built for crammers, visual learners, and any student doing high-level AP concept review. As you read through this book, you will notice that there aren't any practice tests, end-of-chapter drills, or multiple-choice questions. There's also very little test-taking strategy presented in here. Both of those things (practice and strategy) can be found in The Princeton Review's other top-notch AP series—*Cracking.* So if you need a deep dive into AP World History, check out *Cracking the AP World History Exam* at your local bookstore.

ASAP World History is our fast track to understanding the material—like a fantastic set of class notes. We present the most important information that you MUST know (or should know or could know—more on that later) in visually friendly formats such as charts, graphs, and maps, and we even threw a few jokes in there to keep things interesting.

Use this book anytime you want—it's never too late to do some studying (nor is it ever too early). It's small, so you can take it with you anywhere and crack it open while you're waiting for soccer practice to start or for your friend to meet you for a study date or for the library to open.* *ASAP World History* is the perfect study guide for students who need high-level review in addition to their regular review and also for students who perhaps need to cram pre-Exam. Whatever you need it for, you'll find no judgment here!

 Because you camp out in front of it like they are selling concert tickets in there, right? Only kidding.

Who Is This Book For?

This book is for YOU! No matter what kind of student you are, this book is the right one for you. How do you know what kind of student you are? Follow this handy chart to find out!

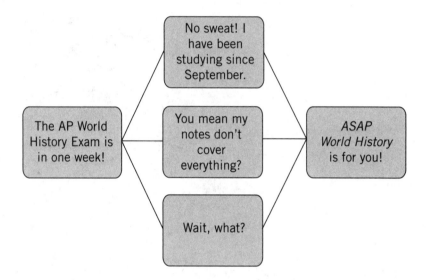

As you can see, this book is meant for every kind of student. Our quick lessons let you focus on the topics you must know, you should know, and you could know—that way, even if the test is tomorrow (!), you can get a little extra study time in, and learn only the material you need.

How Do I Use This Book?

This book is your study tool, so feel free to customize it in whatever way makes the most sense to you, given your available time to prepare. Here are some suggestions:

Target Practice

If you know what topics give you the most trouble, hone in on those chapters or sections.

ASK Away

Answer all of the ASK questions *first*. This will help you to identify any additional tough spots that may need special attention.

Three-Pass System

Start at the very beginning!* Read the book several times from cover to cover, focusing selectively on the MUST content for your first pass, the SHOULD content for your second pass, and finally, the COULD content.

 It's a very good place to start.

Why Are There Icons?

Your standard AP course is designed to be equivalent to a college-level class, and as such, the amount of material that's covered may seem overwhelming. It's certainly admirable to want to learn everything— these are, after all, fascinating subjects. But every student's course load, to say nothing of his or her life, is different, and there isn't always time to memorize every last fact.

To that end, *ASAP World History* doesn't just distill the key information into bite-sized chunks and memorable tables and figures. This book also breaks down the material into three major types of content:

This symbol calls out a section that has MUST KNOW information. This is the core content that is either the most likely to appear in some format on the test or is foundational knowledge that's needed to make sense of other highly tested topics.

This symbol refers to SHOULD KNOW material. This is either content that has been tested in some form before (but not as frequently) or which will help you to deepen your understanding of the surrounding topics. If you're pressed for time, you might just want to skim it, and read only those sections that you feel particularly unfamiliar with.

This symbol indicates COULD KNOW material, but don't just write it off! This material is still within the AP's expansive curriculum, so if you're aiming for a perfect 5, you'll still want to know all of this. That said, this is the information that is least likely to be directly tested, so if the test is just around the corner, you should probably save this material for last.

As you work through the book, you'll also notice a few other types of icons.

The Ask Yourself question is an opportunity to solidify your understanding of the material you've just read. It's also a great way to take these concepts outside of the book and make the sort of real-world connections that you'll need in order to answer the free-response questions on the AP Exam.

There's a reason why people say that "All work and no play" is a bad thing. These jokes and fun facts help to shake your brain up a bit and keep it from just glazing over all of the content—they're a bit like mental speed bumps, there to keep you from going too fast for your own good.

Where Can I Find Other Resources?

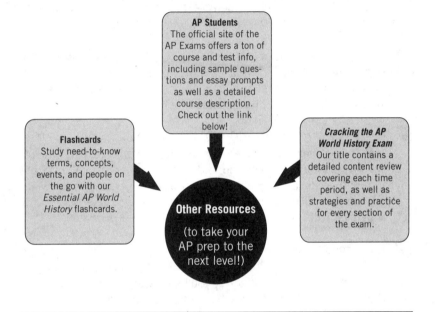

AP Students
The official site of the AP Exams offers a ton of course and test info, including sample questions and essay prompts as well as a detailed course description. Check out the link below!

Flashcards
Study need-to-know terms, concepts, events, and people on the go with our *Essential AP World History* flashcards.

Other Resources
(to take your AP prep to the next level!)

Cracking the AP World History Exam
Our title contains a detailed content review covering each time period, as well as strategies and practice for every section of the exam.

Useful Links

- AP World History Homepage: https://apstudent.collegeboard.org/apcourse/ap-world-history
- Your Student Tools: www.PrincetonReview.com/cracking
  See the "Get More (Free) Content" page at the beginning of this book for step-by-step instructions for registering your book and accessing more materials to boost your test prep.

PERIOD 1

World History to c. 600 B.C.E.

This section explores how nomadic humans created settlements around rivers, which ultimately became the first civilizations. Pay attention to how civilizations in Africa, Asia, and the Americas used similar technologies to establish their cities, as well as how unique religious beliefs helped define their cultures.

Development of Human Civilization

When most people imagine early humans, they immediately picture lone cavemen hunting, traveling, and surviving independently of a society. While there is anthropological evidence of this lifestyle, there are questions you need to ask in order to understand the bigger picture:

- How can civilization be defined?
- How does change occur within a society?
- How are people impacted by, and how do they impact, geography and climate?

More specifically, how and why did humans settle in a particular place, and why was this a logical development? This chapter explores the earliest known human societies that serve as the foundation of modern civilization, as well as the technological and environmental transformations that occurred as these early societies formed.

Nomads in the Paleolithic Era

This period is marked by **nomadic societies** of the earliest humans who traveled from place to place in search of food and shelter. Major developments during this period include spoken language, the ability to control and use fire, and simple stone tools.

Foraging Societies

Foraging societies, or hunter-gatherer clans, were nomadic but had two additional advantages. A clan provided (1) protection and (2) the ability to gather and store more food. This was the beginning of humans living cooperatively in order to survive.

Pastoral Societies

Pastoral societies were characterized by the domestication of animals. This is the first sign of humans settling in one location for a longer period of time. Many pastoral societies used small-scale farming to supplement animal products (usually milk and eggs), as well as semipermanent structures to maintain livestock. Pastoral societies' experimentation with cultivating plants was revolutionary and led to...

The Agricultural Revolution

Agricultural societies developed over thousands of years, from around 8000 B.C.E. to 3000 B.C.E. The **Agricultural Revolution,** or **Neolithic Revolution,** was characterized by

- substantial seasonal farming and domesticated animals
- permanent dwellings with reusable farmland
- tools made of metal and stronger granite, such as hoes and plows, as well as baskets, pottery, and wheels

This was a revolutionary shift in how early humans obtained food: they went from chasing their food to bringing the food to them. People lived closer together and communities formed. This stability allowed the development of traditions and culture as well as social stratification.

What Contributes to the Development of a Civilization?

Specialization of labor is key. For thousands of years, clans were focused on survival, doing whatever they needed to do to find food and shelter. As societies became larger and more complex, it was no longer necessary for everyone in the society to perform every type of job. Instead, people could focus on one type of labor and hone their skills in that area, leading to technological and artistic innovation as well as cultural institutions.

Ask Yourself...

1. How did the Agricultural (Neolithic) Revolution affect the role of women in society?
2. How did the Agricultural Revolution reshape the landscape of the natural environment?
3. Do you see any hints of modern civilization during this time period? If so, what are they?

The Early Civilizations: The Rivers Deliver ❗

Most of the world's early civilizations were located in river valleys. Rivers supplied water and provided transportation. Lowlands surrounding rivers tended to be rich with nutrients. Moreover, rivers were home to animals and plants that could also provide food for people.

Major early civilizations developed and became dominant starting around 3000 to 2000 B.C.E. These civilizations represent the beginning of fully developed societies with traditions, religions, government, economics, and a written history. They were located in Mesopotamia, Egypt, India, and China.

Mesopotamia: "Between the Rivers" !

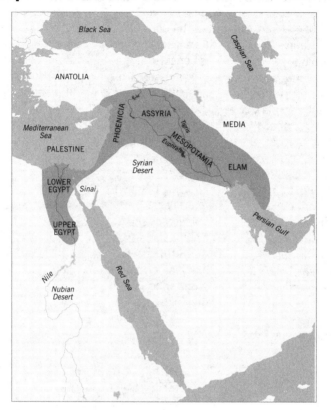

Mesopotamia, part of a larger area of arable land known as the **Fertile Crescent,** literally means "between the rivers." In this case, the rivers were the Tigris and Euphrates Rivers, and a series of ancient civilizations—notably, Sumer, Babylon, and Persia—thrived along their banks. However, the rivers flooded unpredictably, which made the civilizations there unstable.

Some key features of each of these three civilizations are highlighted in the following table.

Sumer 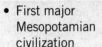	Babylon 💬	Persian Empire 💬
• First major Mesopotamian civilization • Developed **cuneiform**, a form of writing used to set down laws, treaties, and important social and religious customs; the use of cuneiform soon spread to many other parts of the region via trade • Polytheistic (worshipped many gods); built temples called **ziggurats** to appease their gods	• Best known for the **Code of Hammurabi,** which is considered the predecessor of the modern legal code: it distinguished between minor and major offenses and established a sense of justice by applying the laws to everyone • Invaded by the Kassites and then the Hittites, who had learned to use bronze and iron in their weapons	• Arose after the fall of Babylon, which had been rebuilt by **King Nebuchadnezzar** after defeating the Assyrians

Cuneiform is considered the most significant contribution of the Sumerians, who developed this system of writing around 3500–3000 B.C.E. The text here is a list of "gifts from the High and Mighty of Adab to the High Priestess, on the occasion of her election to the temple."

Egypt: Stay Awhile Along the Nile ❗

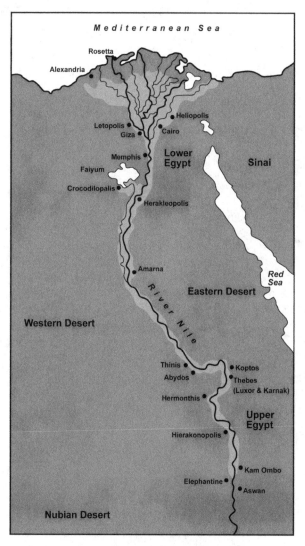

The Egyptian Empire c. 1450 B.C.E.

The ancient Egyptians built their civilization along the Nile River, which, similar to Mesopotamia, made the surrounding soil fertile for agriculture. Unlike the Tigris and Euphrates, however, the Nile overflowed at predictable times throughout the year, making it possible for the Egyptians to follow a stable agricultural cycle.

For many centuries, Egypt was divided into two kingdoms, **Lower Egypt** and **Upper Egypt.**

Lower Egypt
- Northern kingdom named for the lowlands near the mouth of the river
- More advanced than Upper Egypt

The kingdoms were united in 2925 B.C.E. under **King Menes.*** The pharaohs became known as "rulers of the Two Lands," wearing a *pschent,* a headpiece that combined the crowns of the two kingdoms.

Upper Egypt
- Southern kingdom in the highlands
- Agricultural, unlike Lower Egypt, which relied more on hunting and fishing

 There was nothing *mini* about Menes' death. According to legend, he was killed by a hippopotamus.

Egyptian Achievements ❗

Field	What?	So What?
Government	Egypt was united by pharaohs (notably **King Menes**), who led the unified civilization to great wealth and power.	They directed the construction of obelisks and pyramids, enormous tombs for their afterlife.
Writing	Their system of writing consisted of a series of pictures (hieroglyphs) that represented letters and words.	**Hieroglyphics** were used for religion, laws, and even trade.
Economics	Egypt relied heavily on trade, which gave them access to valued luxuries like gold and spices.	Trade brought Egypt into contact with other civilizations.
Religion	Egyptians were polytheistic and focused on the afterlife, where they believed they could take earthly possessions as well as use their bodies.	This belief led to the invention of mummification, a process of preserving dead bodies (though this was available only to the wealthy members of Egyptian society).
Women's Roles	The first female ruler known in history was **Queen Hatshepsut**, who ruled for 22 years and is credited with expanding Egyptian trade.	The relatively high status of women extended beyond royalty; women could buy, sell, and inherit property, for example, and had the right to dissolve their marriages under certain circumstances.*
Social Structure	Hierarchical: • Pharaoh • Priests • Nobles • Merchants; skilled artisans • Peasants	Social mobility was extremely difficult.

Nonetheless, women were expected to be subservient to men and were valued the most when they had children; young girls were not as highly educated as young boys.

Indus Valley Civilization: *Indus*try Ruled ❗

East of Mesopotamia and Egypt, the Indus River Valley civilization grew along the Indus River. It was protected by mountain ranges, and its only connection with the outside world was through the Khyber Pass in the Hindu Kush Mountains. Its two major cities, **Harappa** and **Mohenjo-Daro,** were each home to about 100,000 people—an enormous population by ancient standards. There is strong evidence that these cities were highly developed and master-planned. They had sophisticated waste-water systems, which suggests a strong central government (probably led by a priest-king). From at least 2500 B.C.E. to 1500 B.C.E., the Indus River Valley civilization stretched for some 900 miles along the river.

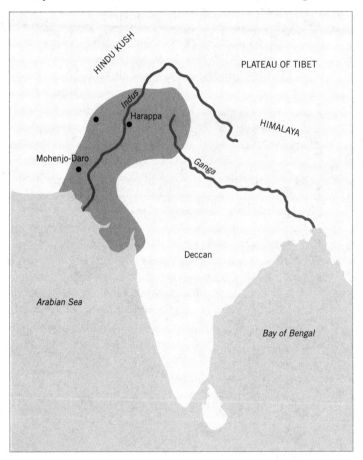

Around 1500 B.C.E., however, the civilization crumbled with the arrival of the **Aryans.**

Aryan Invasion Theory ❶

The Aryan invasion theory is quite controversial, with many Indian nationalists ascribing it to European colonial thinking that refused to attribute Hinduism to nonwhite peoples. While it seems to be a construct of a dark period in the study of history, it is nonetheless tested on the AP World History Exam.

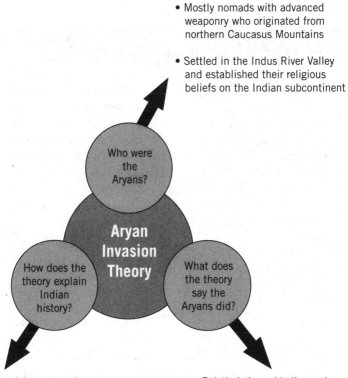

- Mostly nomads with advanced weaponry who originated from northern Caucasus Mountains

- Settled in the Indus River Valley and established their religious beliefs on the Indian subcontinent

Who were the Aryans?

Aryan Invasion Theory

How does the theory explain Indian history?

What does the theory say the Aryans did?

- Aryan social structure began as a three-class system: (1) warriors, (2) priests, and (3) peasants.

- A class of merchants and landowners was added above the peasants, and the **Brahmans** (priests) moved above the warrior class since they were seen as closer to the gods.

- As the system became more engrained, mobility among the castes was prohibited.

- Polytheistic and believers in reincarnation, the Aryans recorded their beliefs and traditions in the **Vedas** and **Upanishads.**

- These early beliefs evolved to form the basis of what became Hinduism.

Early China: Shang on the Hwang ❶

Early Chinese civilization grew along the Hwang Ho River Valley, otherwise known as the Yellow River Valley. Chinese civilization was more isolated than other ancient civilizations, which allowed its culture to remain relatively uninfluenced by western ideas. Religion, for example, developed internally rather than via cultural diffusion. The two main dynasties in early China were the **Shang** and the **Zhou.**

Shang China (c. 1600 B.C.E. to c. 1100 B.C.E.)	Zhou Dynasty (c. 1100 B.C.E. to 256 B.C.E.)
• Strong military power, controlling large parts of northern China • Very limited contact with the rest of the world with the exception of limited trade with Mesopotamia • Ethnocentric culture due to their isolation—they believed they were the center of the world • Industrious—bronze workers, use of wheels, pottery, production of silk	• Longest ruling dynasty in China • Believed in the **Mandate of Heaven,** which deemed that heaven would grant the Zhou power only as long as its rulers governed justly and wisely (and therefore had the blessing of heaven) • Developed a feudal system similar to Europe, in which the king ruled the empire through a noble class • 💬 Formed local **bureaucracies,** whereby the government was organized into different departments, or **bureaus**

The extended family was an important institution in many ancient civilizations, but nowhere was it more important than in Shang China. There, multiple generations of the same family lived in the same household in a **patriarchal** structure (led by the eldest male). Shang religion held that gods controlled all aspects of people's lives; people also believed that they could call on the spirits of their dead ancestors to act as their advocates with the gods. This gave the extended family even more significance.

West Africa: Bantu Migrations ❗

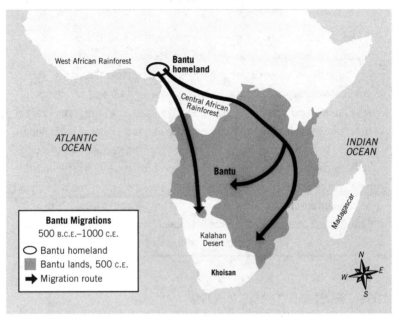

The **Bantu** were tribes of farmers who migrated southeast of the Niger River Valley beginning around 1500 B.C.E. The migrations were prompted by a variety of factors, including

- lack of a livable environment
- the need to find more sustainable food sources
- overpopulation

The migrations continued for some 2,000 years and spread the Bantu language as well as the Bantu people's knowledge of agriculture and metallurgy.

Some Bantu speakers remained along the upper West African coast, where today there are the remains of **Jenne-Jaro**—believed to be the first city in sub-Saharan (south of the Sahara) Africa. Archaeologists believe that this city was unusual in that it was comprised of a collection of individual communities rather than organized hierarchically.

Early Mesoamerica and Andean South America 🛈

Two early civilizations existed in the Americas: the **Olmec** (c. 1500–400 B.C.E.) in modern-day Mexico, and the **Chavin** (c. 900–200 B.C.E.) in the Andes. These civilizations developed similarly to the ones discussed already in this chapter with one notable exception: neither developed in a river valley.

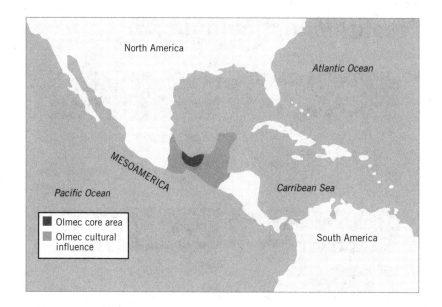

Olmec (c. 1500–400 B.C.E.)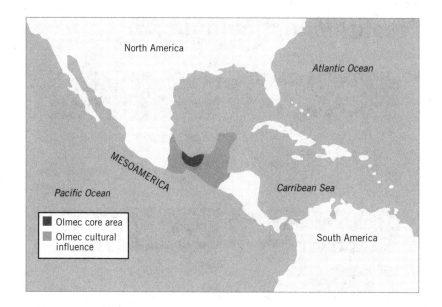

- Supported by food source of corn, beans, and squash
- Mastered irrigation techniques
- Practiced a polytheistic faith
- Developed a system of writing and a calendar

Chavin (c. 900–200 B.C.E.)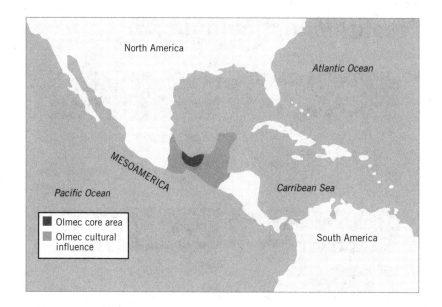

- Were a mostly agricultural community, but supplemented diet with seafood (access to the coast)
- Used the science of metallurgy to make tools and weapons
- Practiced a polytheistic faith

So why bring up these civilizations? First, they demonstrate that the same pattern of civilization development was happening around the globe and not confined to a single region or continent. Second, their existence is proof that river valleys were not essential to the emergence of early civilizations.

Neolithic Technology

Farming Tools (hoes and plows)

Formed by sharpening and shaping hard stones, such as granite

Cooking Tools

Created with pottery and ceramic techniques

Baskets and Nets

Developed through a new process known as weaving

Clothing

Created complex and comfortable clothing through a mastery of textiles

Carts

Improved transportation through the use of the wheel

Boats

Made maritime travel more efficient with the use of sails

 If there had been a stock market for new technologies in the Neolithic Era, it would have attracted many investors.

Related Neolithic Technologies Around the World ∽

Similar technologies emerged around the world, including the following inventions:

Recording Systems	Composite Bow
• Ancient peoples developed systems for counting and recording quantitative information. • In South America, people created **quipus.** • In China, record keepers used a knot system. • In North America, a shell bead system called **wampum** was used.	• Bows used in warfare can be traced to the horse-riding nomads of Central Asia. • Usage spread through trade and cultural contact in China, Egypt, and the Fertile Crescent. • Civilizations in North America as well as other places around the world also created similar weapons independent of contact with central Asian nomads.

The Bronze Age ❗

Perhaps the most significant advance of the Neolithic Era was the knowledge of how to use metals. People figured out how to combine copper with tin to create bronze, a metal harder than its components. This development was so significant that the latter part of the Neolithic Era was named the **Bronze Age**. Bronze was superseded by the discovery of iron.

Period 1: Key Takeaways and Themes 🟡

Technology 🟡

- Settlement and agriculture resulted in the need for basic tools, farming equipment, and weaponry; eventually this made way for other goods (e.g., pottery and textiles) that made life more comfortable.
- Irrigation allowed civilizations to be farther from water sources, control flooding, and make water consistently available. This, in turn, stabilized farming techniques and crops, allowing populations to grow.
- The Bronze Age ushered in metallurgy and the beginning of permanent tools and weapons, allowing people to defend themselves and their territory.

Role of Women 🟡

- In the Paleolithic Era, women were primarily gatherers—an important role, as Paleolithic societies mainly subsisted on vegetables and grains.
- Women were responsible for the socialization of children.
- There is evidence that women were instrumental in the development and spread of the first languages.
- Though men usually led societies, some tribes in Africa were ruled by women.

 Ask Yourself...

1. Based on what you learned in this chapter, how would you define civilization?
2. What were some sources of change during this time period?
3. How did the emergence of civilizations affect the environment and humans' relationship with nature?

PERIOD 2

c. 600 B.C.E. to c. 600 C.E.

The classical civilizations ruled during an extended period in which societies organized themselves based on new religious and governmental systems. Note the similarities in how these empires arose and fell, as well as in the ways far-off cultures were able to interact with one another.

Organization and Reorganization of Human Societies ❗

As societies throughout the world became settled, they looked to innovative governments and followed emerging belief systems to sustain empires that grew larger than any dreamed up by earlier civilizations. Key to this sustenance was a continual flow of cultural diffusion.

The Classical Civilizations: India and China ❗

The four empires in India and China you should know for the AP World History Exam are the Maurya and Gupta (India), and the Qin and Han (China). These empires are closely tied to the religions and philosophies that predominated at the time.

Pay attention to how leadership styles and the use of systems of belief helped carve out bigger and more powerful empires in Asia than had ever been seen up to this point.

Mauryan Empire ❗

Around 330 B.C.E., Alexander the Great conquered the Persian Empire and continued into India (more on this later). A decade later, a new empire arose in India: the **Mauryan Empire**.

Mauryan Empire	
Dates	321 B.C.E.–180 B.C.E.
Belief System	Buddhism
People	**Chandragupta Maurya:** founder of the empire **Ashoka Maurya** (Chandragupta's grandson) • Converted to Buddhism after a particularly bloody battle; preached nonviolence and moderation while managing to bring the empire to its greatest heights
Contributions to the World	Ashoka carved messages on rocks and pillars throughout the empire. These **Rock and Pillar Edicts** reminded Mauryans to live generous and righteous lives. Due to Ashoka's commitment, Buddhism spread beyond India into many parts of Southeast Asia.

Gupta Dynasty 🛈

After Ashoka's death in 232 B.C.E., the Mauryan Empire began to decline rapidly, primarily due to economic problems and pressure from attacks in the northeast. But between 375 and 415 C.E., it experienced a revival: the **Gupta Empire** was born as a more decentralized and smaller empire than its predecessor.

Gupta Empire	
Dates	320 C.E.–550 C.E.
Belief System	Hinduism
People	• **Chandra Gupta the Great** (also known as Chandra Gupta II) founded the empire. • Invasions from the **White Huns** led to the empire's collapse.
Contributions to the World	The Gupta Dynasty is viewed as a golden age for India due to the breakthroughs in art, science, and math. Mathematicians developed the concepts of pi, zero, and a decimal system using numerals 1–9 (which later became known as Arabic numerals).

Qin Dynasty ❶

The Zhou Dynasty ended in a long period of warfare known as the **Period of Warring States,** with rival kingdoms fighting to fill the vacuum of power. The **Qin Dynasty** was victorious.

Qin Dynasty	
Dates	221 B.C.E.–209 B.C.E. (a short-lived but important empire!)
Belief System	Legalism • Strict system of rewards and punishments • Pros: Standardized laws, currencies, weights and measures, and systems of writing • Cons: Under Qin Shi Huang, dissenting scholars were killed and subversive texts were burned.
People	Qin Shi Huang • First emperor of the Qin Dynasty • Unified the warring kingdoms and centralized the government
Contributions to the World	The Qin Dynasty connected separate fortification walls that eventually became the **Great Wall of China.** This is more than just an interesting piece of trivia—it indicates that the empire was incredibly well organized, centralized, and territorial.

Qin Shi Huang used **corvée labor,** a form of slave labor that has been used throughout world history, to build the Great Wall. Corvée is different from the type of slave labor seen in U.S. history. First, corvée laborers were not owned by anyone. Second, such labor was generally for temporary work such as public works projects.

Han Dynasty ❶

The short-lived Qin Dynasty was followed by an empire that would last more than 400 years: the **Han Dynasty**. The Han Dynasty was less repressive than the Qin, but retained the Qin's centralized government administration. The Han also introduced a **civil service system,** based on the teachings of Confucius, in which the highly educated members of society could prove their worthiness for government positions by passing an exam.

Han Dynasty	
Dates	200 B.C.E.–460 C.E.
Belief System	Confucianism
People	**Wudi** (also Wu Ti) 💬 • "Warrior Emperor" • Successful leader who oversaw trade thriving along the Silk Road, encouraged the spread of Buddhism, and fought off attacks from outside groups such as the Huns • Created Confucian academies and selected those who scored highest on an exam for official positions in his government **Xiongnu** 💬 • A large nomadic group from northern Asia who may have been Huns • Invaded territories extending from China to Eastern Europe, but had little success against the Han
Contributions to the World	The Han period saw the invention of paper, calendars, and highly accurate sundials, as well as important strides in navigation, such as the invention of the rudder and compass.

The Classical Civilizations: Mediterranean

As you read this next section, notice the factors that bring about the ups and downs of Greece and Rome. Their histories are a struggle between "strong man" leadership and popular sovereignty.

From approximately 2000 B.C.E. to 500 C.E., two civilizations, Greece and Rome, dominated the Mediterranean region. Western civilization as we know it today essentially began with these two empires. The Mesopotamian civilizations laid the groundwork, but the legacy and lasting influence of the ancient Greeks and the Romans is more pervasive. Perhaps their most important contribution is the concept of representative government, but they (along with the Persians) also made significant contributions to art, architecture, literature, science, and philosophy.

The Persian Empire

The Persians established a big empire that, by 500 B.C.E., stretched from beyond the Nile River Valley in Egypt around the eastern Mediterranean through present-day Turkey and parts of Greece, and then eastward through present-day Afghanistan.

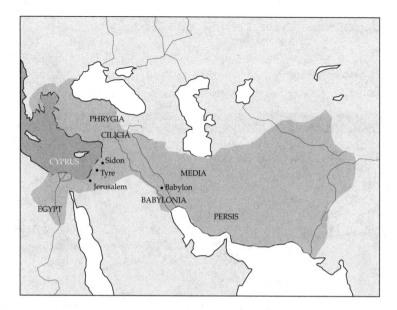

Extent of the Persian Empire

The Persian Empire consisted of three dynasties that reigned during the time period covered by this chapter:

- Achaemenid Empire (550 B.C.E.–330 B.C.E.)
- Parthian Empire (247 B.C.E.–224 C.E.)
- Sassanid Empire (224 C.E.–651 C.E.)

Due to the size of the empire, government administration was delegated locally. The empire was divided into local provinces known as **satrapies,** each of which was overseen by a **satrap,** or governor. A satrapy was allowed to self-govern as long as it paid taxes to the king and provided soldiers when necessary.

One significant achievement of the Persian Empire was its improvements in transportation and communication, which were necessary to maintain such a vast empire. They built a series of long roads, the longest of which was the **Great Royal Road,** which stretched around 1,600 miles from the Persian Gulf to the Aegean Sea.

Lydians, Phoenicians, and Hebrews ❗

Within the Persian Empire, many smaller societies existed and kept their own identities. Among them were the Lydians, Phoenicians, and Hebrews.

	Lydians	Phoenicians	Hebrews
Location	Western Anatolia (modern-day Turkey)	Levant (coastal regions of modern-day Syria, Lebanon, Israel, and Gaza)	Kingdoms of Israel and Judah (modern-day Israel)
Key Trait #1	The Lydians developed coined money for use in trade.	The Phoenicians created city-states along the Mediterranean, thereby dominating maritime trade.	The Hebrews were the first Jews, who—in contrast to previous Fertile Crescent civilizations—were monotheistic.
Key Trait #2	Their monetary system allowed for consistent prices and the ability to put money away for later use.	The Phoenicians created a 22-letter alphabet. The Greeks later adopted this alphabet, which evolved into our current system of letters.	Despite facing oppression (from invasions and enslavement), the Hebrews maintained their identity and persevered in the belief that they were God's chosen people.

Ancient Greece ❶

Because Greece's land is mostly mountainous, there wasn't much possibility for agricultural development on the scale of the ancient river valley civilizations.

Greece's Unusual Geography ❶

Greece is a peninsula between the Ionian Sea and the Aegean Sea that is surrounded by many islands. Its unique geography and limited land provided it with both strategic advantages as well as some security concerns.

- The disjointed topography made innovations in communication, transportation, and governance a necessity.
- The ancient Greeks were always looking to establish colonies abroad to ease overcrowding and obtain raw materials.
- They had to maintain a powerful military to protect themselves from sea invasions as well as to defend their numerous colonies.

Greek Mythology ❷

Like many ancient cultures, the Greeks were polytheistic. However, the richly detailed stories of the gods were unique in one respect: they were believed to possess human failings. They became angry, got drunk, took sides, and had petty arguments. Here are a few of the more well-known Greek gods, which you've probably heard of:

- Aphrodite: goddess of love and beauty
- Apollo: god of the sun
- Ares: god of war
- Artemis: goddess of the hunt
- Athena: goddess of wisdom
- Hades: god of the underworld
- Poseidon: god of the sea
- Zeus: god of the sky (king of the gods)

The richness of Greek culture can be traced back to as early as the 8th century B.C.E. with the composition of two epic poems. **Homer's** the *Illiad* and the *Odyssey* are still regarded as two of Western civilization's masterworks of literature.

The Polis

Ancient Greece was not the unified country that it is today. Instead, it was a collection of city-states. A city-state was known as a **polis**—a collection of people with a common culture, identity, and geographic location. A polis was independent from the other Greek city-states and often found itself in conflict with them. A polis consisted of three groups:

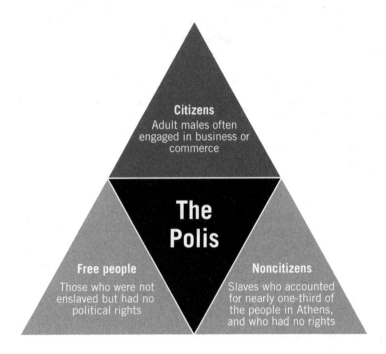

Athens vs. Sparta ❗

The two most important city-states were **Athens** and **Sparta***. There were some key differences between the two.

Athens	Sparta
• Political and cultural center of Greek civilization • Wealthy trade center • Civic decisions opened to all citizens following debates • Saw education as a means to train citizens in the arts, rather than in military skill • Regarded as the world's first democracy (though only adult males with a citizenship designation could participate)	• Agricultural • Highly militaristic • Culture emphasized austerity, discipline, and equality (though not individuality) • Military training for all boys (and even some girls) • Women granted greater equality than women in other city-states

😎 The rivalry between Athens and Sparta would eventually lead to the Peloponnesian War (more on that in a few pages). Here are some other famous rivalries that you *don't* need to know for the AP World History Exam: Red Sox vs. Yankees, Batman vs. Superman, Alexander Hamilton vs. Aaron Burr, Gryffindor vs. Slytherin.

The Persian Wars (499–449 B.C.E.)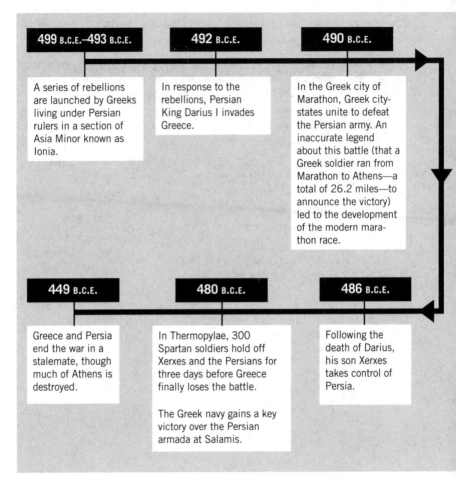

499 B.C.E.–493 B.C.E.

A series of rebellions are launched by Greeks living under Persian rulers in a section of Asia Minor known as Ionia.

492 B.C.E.

In response to the rebellions, Persian King Darius I invades Greece.

490 B.C.E.

In the Greek city of Marathon, Greek city-states unite to defeat the Persian army. An inaccurate legend about this battle (that a Greek soldier ran from Marathon to Athens—a total of 26.2 miles—to announce the victory) led to the development of the modern marathon race.

449 B.C.E.

Greece and Persia end the war in a stalemate, though much of Athens is destroyed.

480 B.C.E.

In Thermopylae, 300 Spartan soldiers hold off Xerxes and the Persians for three days before Greece finally loses the battle.

The Greek navy gains a key victory over the Persian armada at Salamis.

486 B.C.E.

Following the death of Darius, his son Xerxes takes control of Persia.

Athenian Democracy ❶

Athens was unique in its approach to governance. For a time following the Persian Wars, Athens functioned as a direct democracy. That is, all citizens voted on laws directly rather than through representatives.

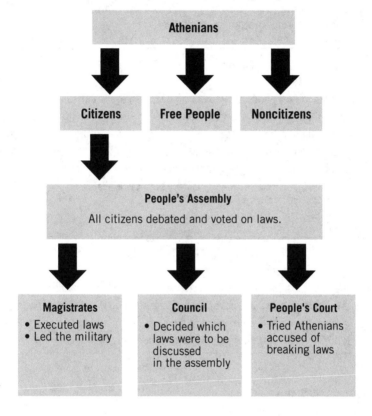

This system of direct democracy was implemented by **Pericles**, a statesman who notably rebuilt Athens following the Persian Wars. (He oversaw the construction of the famous Parthenon.) Pericles built on the groundwork laid centuries earlier by **Draco** and **Solon**, aristocrats who created laws that would foster democratic participation.

Greek Philosophers ❶

Centuries after Homer, Greece found itself in the **Golden Age of Pericles** (480–404 B.C.E.). This Golden Age was Greece's economic, cultural, and artistic zenith. Three of the most famous philosophers, **Socrates, Plato,** and **Aristotle,** lived during this time, and many trace the study of philosophy as it exists today to these three men.

Socrates (470–399 B.C.E.)

Socrates taught philosophy to young people in Greece and influenced them to think critically about the world. He apparently told his audience that "the unexamined life is not worth living." He was charged with riling up young people with objectionable thoughts and ultimately sentenced to death. Given the choice between renouncing his teachings to spare his life or being killed, Socrates chose death.

Plato (c. 428–348 B.C.E.)

Most of what is known about Socrates comes from Plato's writing. Plato was Socrates's most famous student. Plato claimed that the observable world is a mere illusion and that the true "forms" of things can be understood only through careful examination and questioning.

Aristotle (384–322 B.C.E.)

Aristotle was Plato's student. When he was not chosen to succeed Plato in the Academy, Plato's school, Aristotle fled Athens and lived in the woods for a while. He studied nature and came to the realization that Plato was wrong—the observable world is not an illusion, and truth comes from using our senses to experience the world. Aristotle's legacy spread to many academic disciplines, including science.

The Golden Age also saw math and science flourish under Archimedes, Hippocrates, Euclid, and Pythagoras.*

 Ask Yourself...

What other philosophers are you familiar with? Based on their philosophies, would you say they were influenced by these Big Three (Socrates, Plato, and Aristotle)?

The Delian League

Following the destruction caused by the Persian Wars, Pericles established the **Delian League** with other Greek city-states. The Delian League functioned as an alliance to prevent the kind of outside invasions Greece had experienced. A competing alliance, led by Sparta, was known as the **Peloponnesian League.**

You probably remember that last guy's theorem from geometry class.

Peloponnesian Wars (460–446 B.C.E. and 431–404 B.C.E.) ❶

Athens and Sparta, as leaders of their respective alliances, became increasingly fearful and envious of each other's power. After years of increasing tensions, a trade dispute involving the city of Corinth pushed the two city-states and their alliances into the **Peloponnesian Wars,** which are mapped out in the following timeline.

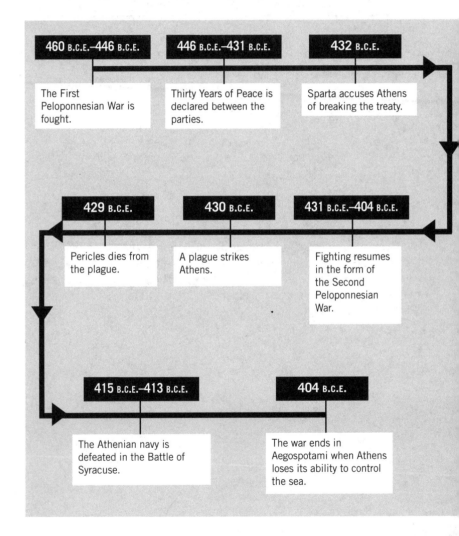

460 B.C.E.–446 B.C.E.

The First Peloponnesian War is fought.

446 B.C.E.–431 B.C.E.

Thirty Years of Peace is declared between the parties.

432 B.C.E.

Sparta accuses Athens of breaking the treaty.

429 B.C.E.

Pericles dies from the plague.

430 B.C.E.

A plague strikes Athens.

431 B.C.E.–404 B.C.E.

Fighting resumes in the form of the Second Peloponnesian War.

415 B.C.E.–413 B.C.E.

The Athenian navy is defeated in the Battle of Syracuse.

404 B.C.E.

The war ends in Aegospotami when Athens loses its ability to control the sea.

Macedonians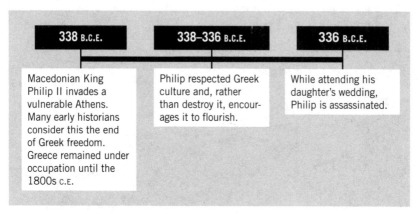

While the Spartans stood victorious following the Peloponnesian War, their war damages and their respect for Athens's contributions to the Persian War kept them from outright destroying the defeated city-state. Instead, a group from the north, the Macedonians, saw the opportunity to conquer Athens.

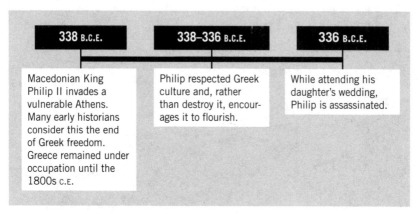

338 B.C.E.	338–336 B.C.E.	336 B.C.E.
Macedonian King Philip II invades a vulnerable Athens. Many early historians consider this the end of Greek freedom. Greece remained under occupation until the 1800s C.E.	Philip respected Greek culture and, rather than destroy it, encourages it to flourish.	While attending his daughter's wedding, Philip is assassinated.

Fortunately for the Macedonians, Philip's empire was left in the capable hands of his son, who later became known as Alexander the Great.

Alexander the Great 🛑

Following the death of Philip II, his son **Alexander the Great,** who happened to be Aristotle's best-known student, continued Macedonian conquests far beyond Greece. Alexander conquered Persia and moved his armies all the way to the Indus River (modern day Pakistan). Upon his return to Macedon in 323 B.C.E., Alexander perished at the age of 33. His generals quickly divided up Alexander's land, which was the largest empire in the world at the time.

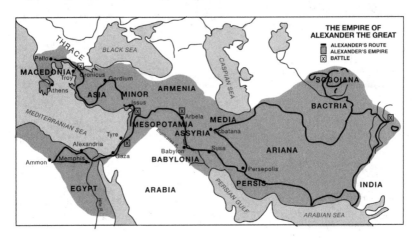

Hellenism 🛑

Greek customs spread far and wide under Alexander, so ancient Greek culture, ideas, and patterns of life lived on beyond the defeats Athens and Sparta suffered following Alexander's death. Three major dynasties evolved from Alexander's conquests: the **Ptolemaic,** the **Seleucid,** and the **Antigonid.**

Dynasty	Location	Accomplishment	Fall
Ptolemaic	Egypt	The wealthiest of the dynasties, its capital, Alexandria, housed a great museum and the Alexandria Library, which contained the most scrolls of any location in the empire (or perhaps the world).	Its downfall was mainly caused by poor leadership. They were slowly absorbed by the Romans, culminating with Augustus Caesar's defeat of Queen Cleopatra.
Seleucid	Near East and Persia	Under this dynasty Hellenism was forced on native populations, creating new Greek cities throughout its lands. This forced Hellenism backfired, as groups, especially the Jews, rebelled against the Seleucids' cultural imperialism.	They suffered defeats by Rome in the 2nd century B.C.E. In 63 B.C.E., Pompey transformed the Seleucid lands into Roman provinces.
Antigonid	Macedon	This dynasty created strategic alliances with the old Greek city-states in its region.	In the 2nd century B.C.E., Rome put an end to the weakening dynasty through a series of wars.

 Ask Yourself...

    1. What was the significance of alliances in ancient Greece?

    2. What factors contributed to the Golden Age of Pericles?

Ancient Rome 🛑

Rome had an ideal location—the Alps in the north and the Mediterranean Sea, which surrounded the Italian Peninsula, protected Rome from attacks from nearly any outside invader lacking an extraordinary armada. However, Rome's isolation did not prevent it from becoming one of the most important trade centers in the world. Its easy access to northern Africa, Palestine, Greece, and the Iberian Peninsula meant access to worldwide markets.

Social Organization 🛑

Roman families centered on the **pater familias**—the eldest male in the family. While women held considerable influence and could even own property, they nonetheless were considered inferior.

The social classes were organized into three groups similar to those of the Greeks:

- **Patricians** (landowning noblemen)
- **Plebeians** (non-landowning freemen)
- **Slaves**

At one point, slaves accounted for one-third of Rome's population, most of whom were natives of conquered territory. Slaves held an assortment of jobs, including farmhands, domestic servants, and even physicians.

The Punic Wars ⚠️

Rome's military dominance was firmly established by the end of the **Punic Wars**, a series of battles that lasted from 264 B.C.E. through 146 B.C.E. Rome's target in the Punic Wars was **Carthage,** a city-state in North Africa, which, like Rome, aspired to have control over the Mediterranean Sea. Check out the following map to see how this all played out.

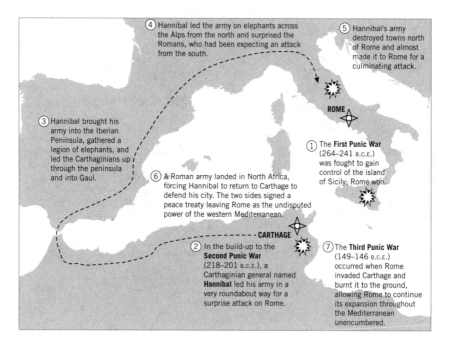

④ Hannibal led the army on elephants across the Alps from the north and surprised the Romans, who had been expecting an attack from the south.

⑤ Hannibal's army destroyed towns north of Rome and almost made it to Rome for a culminating attack.

③ Hannibal brought his army into the Iberian Peninsula, gathered a legion of elephants, and led the Carthaginians up through the peninsula and into Gaul.

① The **First Punic War** (264–241 B.C.E.) was fought to gain control of the island of Sicily; Rome won.

⑥ A Roman army landed in North Africa, forcing Hannibal to return to Carthage to defend his city. The two sides signed a peace treaty leaving Rome as the undisputed power of the western Mediterranean.

② In the build-up to the **Second Punic War** (218–201 B.C.E.), a Carthaginian general named **Hannibal** led his army in a very roundabout way for a surprise attack on Rome.

⑦ The **Third Punic War** (149–146 B.C.E.) occurred when Rome invaded Carthage and burnt it to the ground, allowing Rome to continue its expansion throughout the Mediterranean unencumbered.

CARTHAGE

ROME

The Roman Republic ❶

Originally, Rome functioned as a **republic**: decisions and laws were made by representatives of the people. Notice that this is different from Athens, which had a direct democracy. The Roman Republic functioned with two houses and two executives.

Consuls
- Executive office
- 2 consuls appointed
- 1-year term
- Held veto power over the Assembly

Senate
- Formed by patricians
- Appointed by consuls
- Made foreign and military policy
- Advised the consuls and carried out day-to-day government functions

Assembly
- Formed by patricians and plebians
- Passed laws
- The two major assemblies were made up of tribes (geographic designations) and centuries (soldiers).

The Twelve Tables of Rome 💬

Recognizing the importance of written law, the Roman Republic codified its traditional laws into a group of legal norms known as the **Twelve Tables of Rome**. Here are a few examples of what these laws covered:

Rights of the Accused

Putting to death any man who has not been convicted is forbidden.

Marriage

There shall be no intermarriage between plebeians and patricians.

Inheritance

If anyone dies with no direct heir, the nearest male agnate will inherit the estate.

Slander

If anyone sings or composes an incantation that can cause dishonor or disgrace to another by song, the slanderer shall be clubbed to death.

The Republic Becomes an Empire

One major step toward Rome becoming an empire stemmed from a series of crises in Rome during the 1st century.

- **Crisis #1:** Conquered territories began using slave labor, which displaced rural farmers. The rural farmers moved to the city of Rome, leading to overpopulation and a shortage of jobs.
- **Crisis #2:** Roman currency was devalued, which led to inflation. Plebeians could not afford to buy things they previously could.
- **Crisis #3:** Infighting among the political elite weakened the Senate.

These crises, particularly the third, were exploited by **Julius Caesar**, who held power over southern Gaul (France). He formed an alliance with two other men, creating the **First Triumvirate**.

The First Triumvirate

Caesar
- General and statesman who conquered Gaul
- Received financial support from Crassus on his ascent to power
- Married Egyptian Queen Cleopatra

Pompey
- Known for his military successes from a young age
- Not regarded as an intellectual giant
- Was easily persuaded by the Senate

Crassus
- One of the wealthiest men in Rome
- Used his financial power to gain political influence
- Exhibited incompetence as a military leader

ASAP World History

The First Triumvirate exerted power over the Roman Republic, much to the chagrin of the Senate. With Caesar's followers engaged in an ongoing civil war with the Senate, Pompey's and Crassus's roles became less essential, and they were eventually phased out of the triumvirate. Caesar declared himself "dictator for life" but was assassinated in 44 C.E. by a group of conspiring senators.

The Second Triumvirate

Octavius
- Julius Caesar's grandnephew
- Furthered his power by exploiting the loyalty of Julius Caesar's armies
- First emperor

Mark Antony
- Brought military experience to the triumvirate
- Married Egyptian Queen Cleopatra*

Lepidus
- Two-time consul of the Roman Republic
- Feckless; commonly viewed as the weak link of the Second Triumvirate

Like his great uncle Julius Caesar, **Octavius** positioned himself to become the dominant power in the triumvirate. Soon, a rivalry broke out between him and **Marc Antony** and **Cleopatra**. Octavius emerged victorious, and in 27 C.E. Octavius created the Roman Empire, declaring himself Emperor Augustus Caesar.

 Yup, you read that right. Cleopatra married both Julius Caesar and Mark Antony, so it's safe to say she certainly had a way with Roman generals.

Pax Romana ⚠

Like many civilizations that came before them, such as ancient Greece and the Gupta Empire, the Romans experienced an artistic and economic highpoint. In Rome, this period was known as **Pax Romana** (Roman peace), which lasted from approximately 27 B.C.E. until 180 C.E., as the Roman armies had largely completed the empire's expansion.

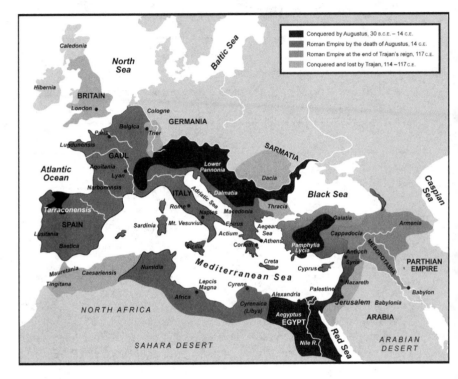

The Height of the Roman Empire

Some key factors that led to the Pax Romana are highlighted in the following table, along with the most significant effects of this period in Roman history.

Causes →	Pax Romana →	Effects
• Empire had grown to its largest extent and did not need further military conquests • Economic stability • Valuable infrastructure through Roman engineering (e.g., **aqueducts** transported water over long distances to provide for the large city populations; quality roads and bridges made travel and trade easier)	• 200 years of peace and prosperity • Diversity of empire allowed for traditional customs of conquered peoples (e.g., Egyptians, Hebrews) to survive	• Increased trade • Flourishing of the arts, literature (Ovid's *Metamorphoses* and Virgil's *Aeneid*), and architecture (Pantheon, Colosseum, Forum) • Increased communication leading to the spread of Christianity, the persecution of both Jews and Christians by Emperor Nero, and ultimately the legalization of Christianity in 313 C.E. with Emperor Constantine's **Edict of Milan**

Empires around the Mediterranean sustained and thrived due to their location on a large body of water that brought in an abundance of trade and some truly significant cultural diffusion. While these empires were built by drawing from their pasts, they allowed for a ripe environment for cultural diffusion to take place.

 Ask Yourself...

What were the benefits and drawbacks of Rome's period as a republic as well as its period as an empire?

The Classical Civilizations: Mesoamerica

Although the Maya are often grouped with later Mesoamerican empires, the Aztec and the Inca, they were actually contemporary with classical Rome, Han China, and Gupta India, and shared some characteristics with these early empires.

The Mayan Civilization

From approximately 300 B.C.E. to 800 C.E., Mayan civilization dominated present-day southern Mexico and parts of Central America. Mayan civilization was similar to many other civilizations at that time in that it was a collection of city-states, but in the Mayans' case these city-states were ruled by the same king.

Here are some key characteristics of the Mayans:

- **Warfare**—War was generally conducted to acquire slaves rather than territory. Slaves were used in large-scale building and agricultural projects. (Human beings were the primary source of labor, as beasts of burden had not yet arrived in the hemisphere.)
- **Calendar**—The Mayan calendar used a number system that included zero, which made it particularly accurate. However, the calendar ended at 2012.
- **Chichen Izta**—This temple, which is similar in design to the Egyptian pyramids, still stands today.
- **Human sacrifice**—The Maya performed bloodletting rituals as an extension of their belief that the gods maintained agricultural cycles in exchange for human sacrifice.
- **Maize**—Mayan religious belief held maize (corn), a dietary staple, in high regard. It was believed that the gods created humans out of maize and water.
- **Big cities**—The Maya built huge cities. Tikal, the most important Mayan political center, may have been populated by as many as 100,000 people.
- **Agricultural techniques**—The Maya utilized the plentiful rainfall and swamp conditions to their advantage with advanced farming techniques, such as the ridged farm system.

While Mayan civilization may seem similar to ancient Greece in its organization of city-states, it actually shares more similarities with the Asian empires discussed earlier in this chapter, particularly in how religion permeated nearly all aspects of society.

The Late Classical Period: Empires Collapse, People Move 🛑

The Late Classical Period (200 C.E. to 600 C.E.) saw the collapse of the greatest civilizations the world had ever known. Some combination of wars (stemming from over-expansion), poor leadership, and bad luck led to the fall of these empires. Yet, even as empires collapsed, cultural diffusion continued.

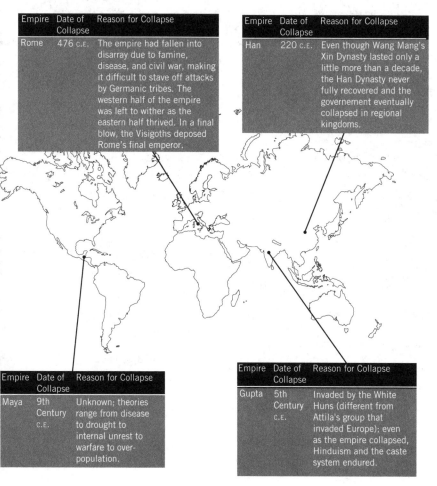

Empire	Date of Collapse	Reason for Collapse
Rome	476 C.E.	The empire had fallen into disarray due to famine, disease, and civil war, making it difficult to stave off attacks by Germanic tribes. The western half of the empire was left to wither as the eastern half thrived. In a final blow, the Visigoths deposed Rome's final emperor.

Empire	Date of Collapse	Reason for Collapse
Han	220 C.E.	Even though Wang Mang's Xin Dynasty lasted only a little more than a decade, the Han Dynasty never fully recovered and the governement eventually collapsed in regional kingdoms.

Empire	Date of Collapse	Reason for Collapse
Maya	9th Century C.E.	Unknown; theories range from disease to drought to internal unrest to warfare to over-population.

Empire	Date of Collapse	Reason for Collapse
Gupta	5th Century C.E.	Invaded by the White Huns (different from Attila's group that invaded Europe); even as the empire collapsed, Hinduism and the caste system endured.

Split of the Roman Empire ❗

The collapse of the Roman Empire stemmed from factors relating to its huge size (such as the cost of maintaining it) combined with weak leaders and a series of epidemics that devastated the population. The split of the Roman Empire into eastern and western sections further weakened the western regions of the empire, including the city of Rome.

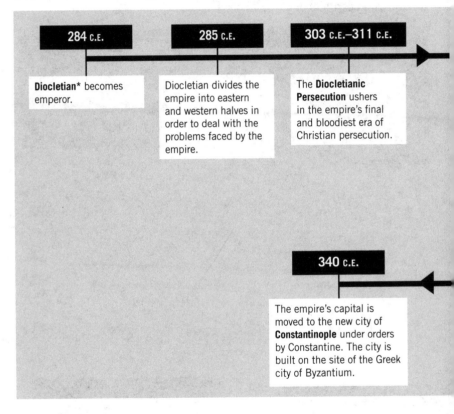

284 C.E.

Diocletian* becomes emperor.

285 C.E.

Diocletian divides the empire into eastern and western halves in order to deal with the problems faced by the empire.

303 C.E.–311 C.E.

The **Diocletianic Persecution** ushers in the empire's final and bloodiest era of Christian persecution.

340 C.E.

The empire's capital is moved to the new city of **Constantinople** under orders by Constantine. The city is built on the site of the Greek city of Byzantium.

Here's a helpful mnemonic device to help you remember Diocletian, Constantine, and these events in history: Diocletian, which starts with a D, divided the empire; Constantine, which starts with a C, moved the capital and legalized Christianity.

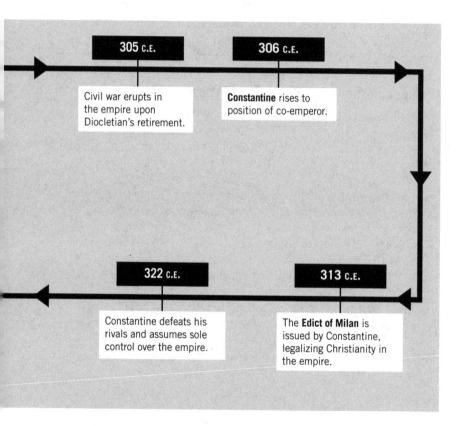

305 c.e.

Civil war erupts in the empire upon Diocletian's retirement.

306 c.e.

Constantine rises to position of co-emperor.

322 c.e.

Constantine defeats his rivals and assumes sole control over the empire.

313 c.e.

The **Edict of Milan** is issued by Constantine, legalizing Christianity in the empire.

After Constantine's death, the eastern half of the empire thrived from its center at Constantinople, while the western half, centered in Rome, continued its downward spiral.

The Visigoths

The Visigoths were a Germanic tribe, which, along with the Vandals, Anglo-Saxons, and Huns, among others, are credited with sacking Rome. The Visigoths were unique in their adoption of Roman law and Christianity. In a way, they were forced to invade the city of Rome—the Huns were attacking the Visigoths from the east, and the Visigoths had no choice but to retreat into Rome.

Collapse of the Xin, Restoration of the Han

The Han Dynasty was briefly interrupted by the Xin Dynasty when **Wang Mang** (9 c.e.–23 c.e.) overthrew the ruling Liu family. A respected government official, Wang Mang did not seem to have much luck ruling the Xin Dynasty.

- **Economy**—Wang Mang's attempted reforms of land ownership and the currency were unsuccessful and caused chaos in the local economy among both the rich and poor.
- **Military**—Waging war on the edges of the empire led to conscription of a resentful population and heavy taxation of landowners, which forced them to pay farmers less money for more work.
- **Natural Disasters**—Famines, devastating floods along the Yellow River, and increasing prices added to resentment and fueled peasant uprisings.

Wang Mang's death in 23 c.e. closed out the short-lived Xin Dynasty, and the Han was restored.

Cultural Diffusion Along the Silk Road, 200 c.e.–600 c.e. !

Around the same time that major empires began to collapse, the known world was becoming an increasingly smaller place. Trade routes were flourishing, bringing cultures, religions, and invading tribes into constant contact with each other. Major trade routes over land, like the **Silk Road** (shown in the map below) from China to the Roman Empire, took months to traverse.

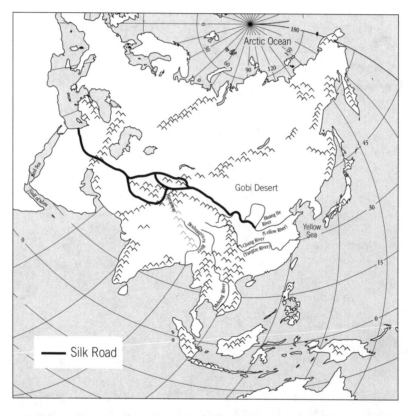

Major Travelers Along the Silk Road		
Goods	• Cotton • Gems • Spices	• Silk • Horses	• Gunpowder • Paper
Ideas	• Buddhism	• Christianity	• Arabic numerals
Disease	• Black Death	• Measles	• Small pox

The increased trade of the Late Classical Period revolutionized the societies that benefited from the Silk Road by introducing new technologies.

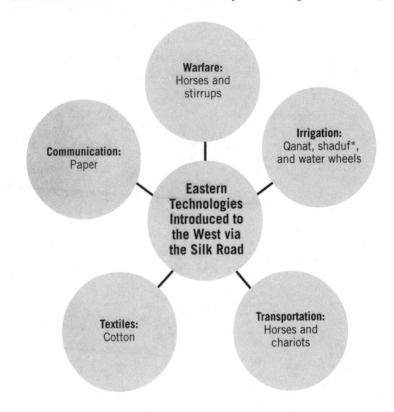

 Ask Yourself...

1. What conclusions can you make about why, in general, empires collapse?
2. What relationship do you see between the end of these major empires and the beginnings of cross-cultural interactions?

 Qan-what? Sha-huh? A qanat is an underground tunnel system for extracting and transporting water, which was used in hot, arid climates. A shaduf is a manually operated device for lifting water. It was used by the ancient Egyptians and is still used today in Egypt, India, and other countries.

Changes and Continuities in the Role of Women ❗

An unfortunate fact of sedentary societies is that women lose power as people settle down. Still, women maintained power within the private sphere. By managing their households and taking responsibility for children's education, wives and mothers were often an unrecognized power.

Women's Status in Ancient Societies		
Rome/Greece	India	China
Strict patriarchal social divisions	Strict patriarchal caste system	Strict Confucian social order and guidelines for virtuous behavior
Little land ownership	Not allowed to inherit property	Only sons inherit property
High literacy among upper-class women	Forbidden to read sacred texts	Upper-class women educated in arts and literature; all women educated in virtues
Granted citizenship in Sparta	No citizenship	No citizenship
Could own businesses (especially widows)	Needed large dowry; widows could not remarry	Arranged marriages; widows permitted to remarry
Could be priestesses (or, later, nuns)	Could not achieve *moksha**	Buddhist convents; Daoism promoted male and female equality

Moksha is the release from the cycle of rebirth, and thus the attainment of peace and fulfillment for the soul. See page 56 for more on this concept.

Major Belief Systems Through 600 C.E. !

Many religions that still exist today took shape in the ancient world. Though these belief systems have evolved over the years, the centrality of these religions to the study of world history cannot be overstated. Their impact can be seen in social, political, and even military developments. This section focuses on the major characteristics of these belief systems that may appear on the AP World History Exam.

Belief Systems Originating in Asia Before 600 c.e.		
Middle East	**South Asia**	**East Asia**
Zoroastrianism	Hinduism	Confucianism
Judaism	Buddhism	Daoism
Christianity		Legalism

Polytheism !

The emergence of monotheistic belief systems is a relatively new one in world history. For millennia before Zoroastrianism or Judaism, humans were **polytheistic,** worshipping a variety of gods, including ancestors and animals. Some well-known polytheistic cultures are the Mesopotamian empires (e.g., Sumer) and Mediterranean empires (e.g., Greece), as well as Hinduism and traditional Chinese belief systems further east in Asia.

Prehistoric Belief Systems

Many polytheistic religions have their roots in prehistoric religious practices, which also influenced some of the later belief systems mentioned in this chapter.

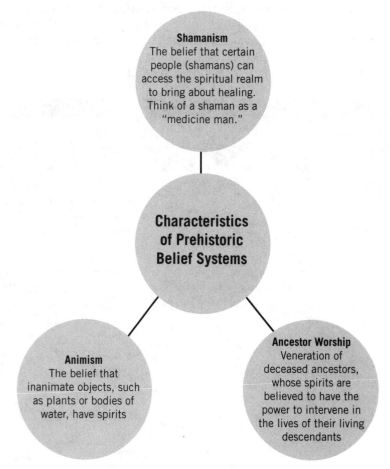

Shamanism
The belief that certain people (shamans) can access the spiritual realm to bring about healing. Think of a shaman as a "medicine man."

Characteristics of Prehistoric Belief Systems

Animism
The belief that inanimate objects, such as plants or bodies of water, have spirits

Ancestor Worship
Veneration of deceased ancestors, whose spirits are believed to have the power to intervene in the lives of their living descendants

 Ask Yourself...

Can you think of any ways that these characteristics have influenced some of the world's major religions?

South Asian Belief Systems ⚠

Both **Hinduism** and **Buddhism** originated on the Indian subcontinent. Scholars used to attribute the emergence of Hinduism to the Aryans, an outside group who invaded the subcontinent. However, modern scholarship now points to the people of South Asia as the first to practice this religion. Buddhism emerged from Hinduism, in no small part as a reaction to Hinduism's social class system, the **caste system.** Siddhartha Gautama, later known as the **Buddha,** taught that spiritual highness, or nirvana, could be achieved by anyone, regardless of caste.

	Hinduism	Buddhism
Origin	c. 1500 B.C.E.	c. 500 B.C.E.
Core Beliefs	One supreme force called *Brahma* exists and takes the form of many gods, such as Vishnu and Shiva.	Four Noble Truths: • Life is suffering. • Desire causes suffering. • This suffering can end. • There is a path to end this suffering.
Spiritual Goal	*Moksha*, or unification with *Brahma*. This is the highest state of being for Hindus and creates internal peace and release of the soul.	• *Nirvana*, which means to extinguish desire. Some Buddhists think of this as a place in the afterlife and some think of it as a state of being. • *Bodhisattvas*, for instance, are Buddhists who have achieved *nirvana* but have chosen to remain on Earth to help others.

	Hinduism	Buddhism
How to Achieve Spiritual Goal	• *Moksha* takes many lifetimes and therefore Hindus believe in reincarnation, or a literal rebirth. • By following the rules and expectations of one's caste, *dharma*, one can move closer to unification with *Brahma* (or move backward due to bad living).	• To reach *nirvana*, one must get rid of desire. • Buddhism prescribes the **Eightfold Path,** a system of good living that Buddhists incorporate into everyday life: right views, right aspirations, right speech, right conduct, right livelihood, right endeavor, right mindfulness, and right meditation. • As with Hinduism, this may take several lifetimes. Buddhists likewise believe in reincarnation.
Sacred Text	*Vedas* and *Upanishads* are guides for many Hindus. These books contain prayers and the origin stories.	There is not one specific sacred text, but the Pali Canon offers the words of the Buddha. Collections of *sutras,* or Buddhist scriptures, are also read by practitioners.

Buddhist Sects 💬

In the early centuries of Buddhism, the religion traveled north and east into other parts of Asia. Hinduism remained the major religion of India, but Buddhism continued to grow elsewhere, splitting into a variety of sects, two of the main ones being **Theravada** and **Mahayna**.

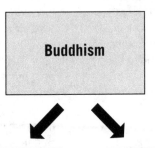

Buddhism

Theravada Buddhism*

This sect attempts to emulate the actions of the original Buddha as closely as possible. Due to this goal, it tends to have quite a strict interpretation of Buddhism and does not spread so easily. Most practitioners are located in Sri Lanka and Thailand.

Mahayana Buddhism

This sect is also known as the "Big Vehicle" because of the distance it spread north into Asia. It spread more easily than Theravada Buddhism due to its ability to absorb local traditions into its practices, even if those practices do not directly emulate the original Buddha.

Some sources may also refer to Theravada Buddhism as Hinayana, which is an earlier incarnation of the sect.

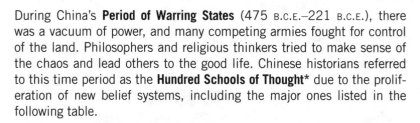

Hindu and Buddhist Art

Much of the art of Hinduism and Buddhism is rife with symbols that are intended to teach the proper practice and understanding of the religions. For example, a Buddha statue typically contains symbols such as a lotus flower at the Buddha's feet, representing enlightenment, as well as various hand gestures, known as *mudras*. Mudras can represent ideas such as meditation or generosity.

East Asian Belief Systems ❗

During China's **Period of Warring States** (475 B.C.E.–221 B.C.E.), there was a vacuum of power, and many competing armies fought for control of the land. Philosophers and religious thinkers tried to make sense of the chaos and lead others to the good life. Chinese historians referred to this time period as the **Hundred Schools of Thought*** due to the proliferation of new belief systems, including the major ones listed in the following table.

Even though Buddhism began in India, it is no accident that it quickly took hold in China during the Hundred Schools of Thought.

	Confucianism	Daoism	Legalism
Origin	5th century B.C.E.	4th century B.C.E.	3rd century B.C.E.
Core Beliefs	Life is best when people follow the order of proper relationships.	Life is best when people follow the order of the Dao (understood by many to be the natural flow of nature).	Life is best when people follow orders.
Spiritual Goal	To achieve balance and harmony through healthy, interpersonal relationships	To live as one with the Dao	To achieve order in society through a strict system of rewards and punishments (not a spiritual goal)
How to Achieve Spiritual Goal	Confucians follow several key values. Here are three examples: • *Ren*—a sense of humanity, kindness, and benevolence • *Li*—a sense of propriety, courtesy, respect, and deference to elders • *Xiao*—filial piety, or respect for family obligations	Wuwei is the process of living effortlessly in the flow of the Dao while disengaging from worldly affairs. People experience hardships when they try to act contrary to the natural course of things.	Follow laws and act in accordance with the goals of an orderly society.
Sacred Text	*The Analects* by Confucius	*The Dao De Jing* by Laozi	*Han Feizi* by Han Fei

Middle Eastern Belief Systems ❶

Some of the best-known monotheistic belief systems originated in the Middle East and Persia.

	Zoroastrianism	Judaism	Christianity
Origin	2nd century B.C.E.	6th century B.C.E.	1st century C.E.
Core Beliefs	Ahura Mazda, the main god of good and truth, tries to lead his followers into overcoming the forces of evil and chaos.	There is one God. God has a covenant, or an agreement, with his people.	There is one God. Jesus is both God and the Son of God who was sent to Earth to die in order to save humanity from its sins.
Spiritual Goal	Through its actions, humanity must ensure that order survives the forces of evil.	To carry out humans' end of the covenant with God	Ascension into heaven; eternal salvation
How to Achieve Spiritual Goal	Individual actions of a person through his or her life determine the spiritual salvation of the soul. When chaos is removed from the Universe, humans will transcend depending on their behaviors in their lifetimes.	Live according to the laws of the Torah.	Following the teachings of Jesus, which are primarily to love God and one's neighbor.
Sacred Text	The Avesta	The Hebrew Scriptures. The five books of the Torah are the most essential of these ancient Hebrew texts.	The Bible. The Christian Bible consists of the Hebrew texts, known to Christians as the Old Testament, along with the Gospels, letters from Paul, and other texts, which is collectively known as the New Testament.

c. 600 B.C.E. to c. 600 C.E.

Spread of Zoroastrianism

While the founding of Zoroastrianism is attributed to Iranian prophet Zoroaster, much of its popularity among the Iranian people can be attributed to the **Sassanid Empire,** which made it the state religion.

Paul the Apostle and Early Christianity

Paul the Apostle lived in the Roman Empire during the time of Jesus, but they never met during Jesus's lifetime. Born Saul of Tarsus, Paul was said to have persecuted some of the first followers of Jesus until he had a vision of the Christ figure and became a follower himself. Paul established churches along the Mediterranean coast of Europe. Since he preached in the Greek-speaking world as well as among Jews, he had to overcome some of the conflicts between the two cultures. Paul wrote letters, or epistles, to these distant churches to address concerns and questions of people who heard his message. These letters are some of the earliest Christian texts and many are included in the New Testament of the Bible.

Just as Buddhists and Daoists turned to spirituality during the Period of Warring States, early Christians adopted Christian **monasticism** to focus on spiritual aims amid the chaos of an intolerant Roman Empire.

Christian Art

Much Christian art has been used over the centuries for devotional purposes. Subjects typically include Jesus, saints (venerated holy figures in Christianity), and biblical stories. While symbolism is far from absent from Christian art, Christian artists, particularly in Western Europe, have long delivered more realistic depictions of their subjects than have those of Hinduism and other eastern religions.

 Ask Yourself...

1. How did each of the belief systems reflect the needs of the communities who originally practiced them?
2. What similarities exist among the belief systems mentioned in this section?

Period 2: Key Takeaways and Themes ❗

We covered a lot of material in this chapter. The first half focused largely on the governing styles and military events that led to the rise of some of the world's greatest empires. The second half outlined the emerging religious and philosophical systems of the period. It is critical to see these as two sides of the same coin. These belief systems touched every segment of society (e.g., the Hindu caste system in India), and governments often used this to their advantage to achieve legitimacy (e.g., Christianity in the late Roman Empire and Legalism under the Qin Dynasty). As trade flourished, these belief systems spread and empires grew.

PERIOD 3

c. 600 C.E.
to c. 1450

This period is defined by the new states that arose following the collapse of the classical civilizations, as well as by the interactions—both positive and negative—between these new states. This period is also one of tremendous growth in long-distance trade. While Europe spent these 850 years decentralizing, trade and military conflicts led to the expansion of Middle Eastern and Chinese empires.

The Rise of Islam 🔊

In the 7th century c.e., a new faith took hold in the Middle East. This faith, called **Islam,** was monotheistic, like Judaism and Christianity.*

Islam Essentials	
The Followers	Muslims
The Founder	The prophet **Muhammad**
The Sacred Text	**Qur'an** (Muslims believe this text is a revelation from God delivered to Muhammad.)
The Place	• Founded in Saudi Arabia and spread worldwide; the Islamic practicing world is known as **Dar al Islam** • Flourished in the **Levant** (present-day Israel, Jordan, Lebanon, and points north and south). Muslims battled with Christians in the Crusades for control of the Levant.

Origins of Islam 🔊

In fact, Islam recognizes the same god as Judaism and Christianity.

Growing up in **Mecca,** Muhammad was exposed to many religions, due in part to Mecca's location on trade routes between the Mediterranean Sea and the Indian Ocean. Mecca was a pilgrimage destination for many religious believers, many of whom were polytheistic. Profiteers took advantage of this by setting up shop and making money off the travelers.

When he began preaching the monotheistic religion of Islam, Muhammad came into conflict with the leaders of Mecca. Persecuted and threatened with death, Muhammad and his followers fled to Medina in 622 c.e. This event is known as the **hijra** (which also marks year 1 on the Muslim calendar).

Muhammad and his followers found support in Medina (see the map on the previous page), and in 630 c.e., Muhammad returned to Mecca and destroyed the pagan shrines—except for the Ka'bah, which became a focal point of Islamic pilgrimage to Mecca.

Islamic Practice 🔴

Muslims believe that salvation is achieved through submission to the will of Allah (the Arabic word for God), and that this can be accomplished through the **Five Pillars of Islam**. Islam is also guided by the concept of **jihad**, which means "to struggle." This has historically referred to both the struggle to be a better Muslim and the struggle against nonbelievers.

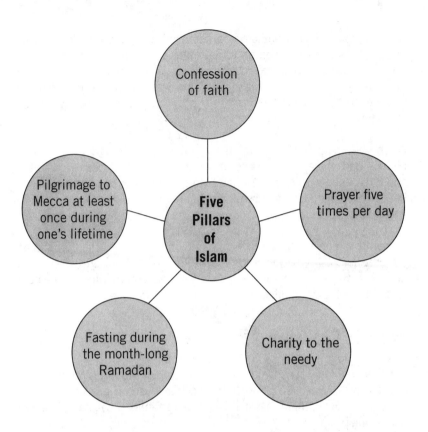

Islam After Muhammad

When Muhammad died unexpectedly in 632 c.e., **Abu Bakr**, one of his first followers in Mecca, became **caliph**, a position that acts as both an emperor and a religious leader. In this respect, his empire was a **theocracy**, a government ruled by immediate divine governance or by officials who are regarded as divinely guided. Abu Bakr's empire was known as a **caliphate.** As Islam began to exist as a religion independent of this first caliphate, tensions emerged around the issue of succession.

The four caliphs were Abu Bakr, Umar, Uthman, and Ali. The last of the four, Ali, was assassinated and succeeded by his son, Hasan. However, because Ali was not a blood relative of Muhammad (he married Muhammad's daughter), many Muslims disagreed about whether his successors should automatically be chosen as leaders. Eventually, the Muslims split into two camps, **Shiite** and **Sunni.**

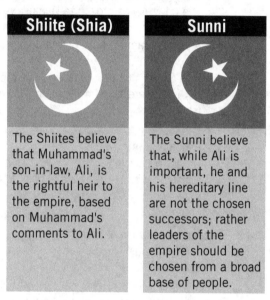

Shiite (Shia)	Sunni
The Shiites believe that Muhammad's son-in-law, Ali, is the rightful heir to the empire, based on Muhammad's comments to Ali.	The Sunni believe that, while Ali is important, he and his hereditary line are not the chosen successors; rather leaders of the empire should be chosen from a broad base of people.

Caliphates ❗

Following the first four caliphs, Hasan relinquished his title under pressure from a prominent family in Mecca. Thus began the **Umayyad Dynasty**, the first of Islam's two early golden ages.

Umayyad Dynasty ❶

Dates	661–750 C.E.
Characteristics	• The dynasty was largely secular (not theocratic). • The capital was moved to Damascus while Mecca remained the spiritual center. • Arabic became the official language of the government. • Non-Muslim conquered peoples were tolerated, but they were taxed unless they converted to Islam.
Accomplishments	• Expanded into territory through northern Africa and into Spain • Ruled the southern Iberian Peninsula city of Córdoba, which became one of the richest and most sophisticated cities in Europe • 💬 Sufism (the mystic practice of Islam) emerged as a reaction against the secularism of the dynasty. Sufis became effective missionaries due to their encouraging others to practice their own way of revering Allah. • 💬 Built the **Dome of the Rock** (a sacred mosque) on Temple Mount in Jerusalem
Fall	As the Shia and non-Arab Muslims began to assert themselves, the Umayyad Dynasty went into decline. Its loss in a battle against Abu al-Abbas, a descendant of Muhammad's uncle, meant the end of the dynasty.

In 732 C.E., the Islamic Empire began to make a move on Europe, by way of the Iberian Peninsula (Spain). At the time, Muslims held most of the Iberian Peninsula and southern parts of Italy, while Christians dominated all the regions to the north. **Charles Martel** (686–741 C.E.), a Frankish leader, stopped the Muslim advance in its tracks as it tried to advance toward Paris, and so the Islamic Empire never flourished in Europe beyond parts of Spain and southern Italy.

Abbasid Dynasty ❶

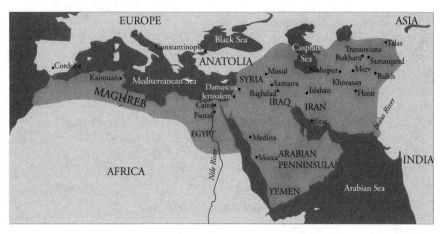

The Abbasid Caliphate c. 850 c.e.

The following table outlines the important characteristics and accomplishments of the Abbasid Caliphate. It also presents reasons for its failure.

Dates	• 750–1258 c.e.
Characteristics	• Cosmopolitan • Focused on expansion • Tolerant of local customs (though Jews and Christians in the Levant were often persecuted), but nonetheless encouraged conversion to Islam
Accomplishments	• Grew capital city **Baghdad** into one of the great cultural centers of the world, where arts and sciences flourished • Introduced the concept of credit, which relieved the burden (and danger) of carrying coins • Learned from T'ang Chinese how to make paper • Built libraries and a university, which collected scholarship from around the world • Preserved learning from the ancient Greeks and Romans that was rejected by European Christians, who had little use for what they considered pagan texts

| **Fall** | <ul><li>Destabilization resulted due to increasing sectarian and ethic rivalries in the expanding empire.</li><li>Turkish warrior slaves revolted and established a new capital at Samarra in central Iraq.</li><li>Rival groups carved out pieces of the empire: Shia in northern Iran, **Seljuk Turks**, and nomadic Sunnis.</li><li>In 1258 during the Crusades, **Mongol** invasions overran the empire, destroying Baghdad.</li><li>Abbasid citizens fled to Egypt, intact but powerless.</li><li>**Ottoman Turks** reunited Egypt, Syria, and Arabia in a new Islamic state that would last until 1918.</li></ul> |

Islamic Advancements

In addition to trade, manufacturing played an important role in the expansion of the Islamic empire. Steel, for example, was produced for use in swords. There were also many achievements in the fields of medicine and mathematics, especially algebra. **Muhammad al-Razi** published a massive medical encyclopedia that was unlike anything compiled before it.

Indian Ocean Trade

Throughout this period, Persians and Arabs dominated **Indian Ocean Trade**. Their routes connected ports in western India to ports in the Persian Gulf, which in turn were connected to ports in eastern Africa.

Key Facts About Indian Ocean Trade

- Travel was often dependent on the monsoon winds.
- Sailors frequently married the local women at the end of their trade routes, which resulted in mixing of cultures and languages.

Women and Islam

While the emergence of Islam in some ways increased rights for women in Arabia, in other ways women remained stifled throughout the Middle Ages.

Before the Qur'an	What the Qur'an Changed	Medieval Islamic Society
• In Arabia, women were viewed as property to men. • Men could keep a woman's dowry after divorcing her. • Baby girls were seen as less valuable than baby boys, leading to infanticide.	• Women, while still subservient to men, had some legal rights. • Women were seen as equal before Allah. • Men had to return a dowry after divorce. • Infanticide was forbidden. • Women gained influence in the home and, occasionally, outside of it. (Muhammad's wife, Khadija, had been a successful businesswoman.)	• Men could have as many as four wives as long as he could support them and treated them equally. • Women had to be faithful to one man. • Women's testimony in court was given only half the weight of a man's. • Women sometimes had to be veiled in public (a Mesopotamian and Persian custom that was adopted by Islam).

 Ask Yourself...

1. How did trade routes impact the development of Islam?
2. What impact did Islam have on arts and sciences?

Developments in Europe and the Byzantine Empire ❗

Developments in Europe and points east became quite complicated during the **Middle Ages**, the period after the fall of Rome and before the Renaissance. As you might recall from the last chapter, the Roman Empire, and eventually Christianity, split into two factions. The eastern Roman Empire, centered in Constantinople, became the highly centralized government known as the **Byzantine Empire**; in the west, the empire collapsed entirely, though Christianity retained a strong foothold.

Byzantine Empire ❗

Throughout the Middle Ages, the Byzantine Empire had certain characteristics that distinguished the region from Western Europe.

- Used the Greek language
- Had its own architecture with distinctive domes
- Shared similarities with Eastern cultures such as Persia
- Had emperors who ruled by absolute authority
- Achieved thriving industries by trading with foreign countries (silk production came to the Byzantine Empire via China)
- Used coined money
- Practiced its own brand of Christianity known as **Orthodox Christianity**

Despite these differences, under Emperor **Justinian**, who reigned from 527–565 C.E., the former glory and unity of the Roman Empire was somewhat restored in Constantinople. Christian Constantinople and Islamic Baghdad rivaled each other for cultural supremacy. Justinian even attempted to regain the land of the Roman Empire, but 20 years of wars with the Ostrogoths in Italy prevented him from achieving this goal (all the while bankrupting his coffers).

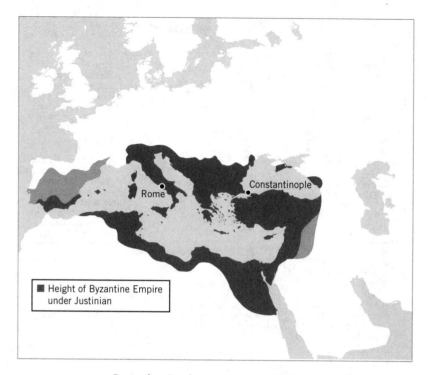

Byzantine Empire at Its Height, 564 c.e.

Law Under Justinian 💬

One of Justinian's notable contributions was the codification of Roman law, known informally as **Justinianic Code**. This kept ancient Roman legal codes alive, though Justinian's final product added laws of his own. The first major test of Justinian's legal backbone came in 532 c.e. in what became known as the Nika riots. See the timeline on the next page.

The Nika Riots

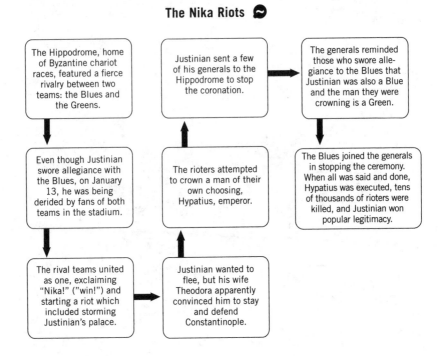

The Hippodrome, home of Byzantine chariot races, featured a fierce rivalry between two teams: the Blues and the Greens.

Even though Justinian swore allegiance with the Blues, on January 13, he was being derided by fans of both teams in the stadium.

The rival teams united as one, exclaiming "Nika!" ("win!") and starting a riot which included storming Justinian's palace.

Justinian wanted to flee, but his wife Theodora apparently convinced him to stay and defend Constantinople.

The rioters attempted to crown a man of their own choosing, Hypatius, emperor.

Justinian sent a few of his generals to the Hippodrome to stop the coronation.

The generals reminded those who swore allegiance to the Blues that Justinian was also a Blue and the man they were crowning is a Green.

The Blues joined the generals in stopping the ceremony. When all was said and done, Hypatius was executed, tens of thousands of rioters were killed, and Justinian won popular legitimacy.

Byzantine Art

While the Byzantines (or more specifically, Justinian) saw themselves as the natural heir to the Roman Empire, their art had its own distinct style. One example is **mosaics**, which were used to decorate churches with elaborate tile patterns. The image below, a representation of Justinian, is one of the most well-known examples of a mosaic.

Hagia Sophia 💬

To rebuild Constantinople from the Nika riots, Justinian commissioned the construction of many buildings and churches, notably a church known as the **Hagia Sophia**. Replicating many of the classical architectural techniques (though much more enormous in scale), the Hagia Sophia helped Justinian establish what he considered a new Roman Empire.

Religion and State in Roman Catholicism and Christian Orthodoxy ❗

The **East-West Schism** of 1054 officially separated Christianity into two separate religions. While the Byzantine Empire was far more centralized than Western Europe—which was largely a collection of tribal regions and kingdoms during the Middle Ages—the reverse is true of their religions. The Roman Church in the West was far more centralized.

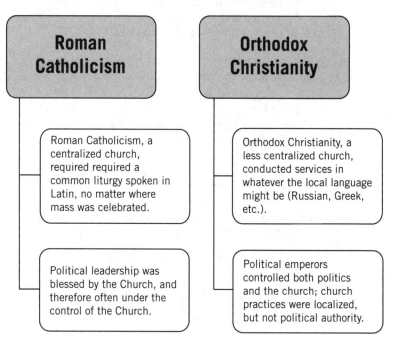

Roman Catholicism

Roman Catholicism, a centralized church, required required a common liturgy spoken in Latin, no matter where mass was celebrated.

Political leadership was blessed by the Church, and therefore often under the control of the Church.

Orthodox Christianity

Orthodox Christianity, a less centralized church, conducted services in whatever the local language might be (Russian, Greek, etc.).

Political emperors controlled both politics and the church; church practices were localized, but not political authority.

Western Europe in the Middle Ages

Western Europe was not as unified as the Byzantine Empire, and therefore understanding the political layout of Western Europe is a bit more complicated. Instead of a single emperor, there were multiple kingdoms, some of which operated under a social, economic, and political system known as **feudalism**. Feudalism was a strict hierarchy with almost no opportunity for upward mobility due to a system of **primogeniture**, which passed down land and titles to the eldest son.

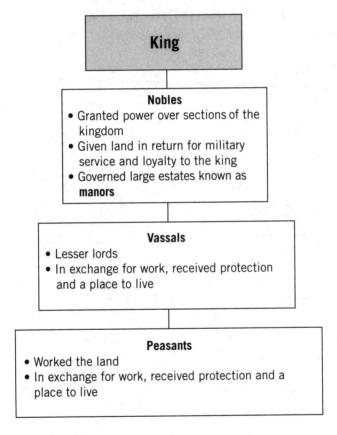

King

Nobles
- Granted power over sections of the kingdom
- Given land in return for military service and loyalty to the king
- Governed large estates known as **manors**

Vassals
- Lesser lords
- In exchange for work, received protection and a place to live

Peasants
- Worked the land
- In exchange for work, received protection and a place to live

Agricultural Breakthroughs 💬

Many manors were self-sufficient, producing all of their own food, clothing, tools, and other goods. This self-sufficiency was made possible by scientific and technological advances during this period, including the following:

- **Three-field system**—Involved the rotation of three fields—one for the fall harvest, one for spring, and one unseeded field—in order to replenish nutrients in the soil
- **Horse collar**—A harness fitted around a horse's neck in order to attach to a plow or wagon, thereby making field preparation and harvest collection more efficient

Merchants in the Feudal System ❗

The opportunity for social climbing eventually presented itself in the form of **mercantilism**. As trade increased in importance, towns with wealthy merchants popped up near the manors, which were no longer the most powerful entities in medieval Europe. Middle-class merchants known as **burghers** became politically powerful, ultimately using their economic leverage to limit the reach of vassals and lords. Eventually, the towns formed alliances with one another. The most famous alliance was the **Hanseatic League**. Established in 1358, it controlled trade throughout much of northern Europe, as shown on the map on the next page.

Trade Routes of the Hanseatic League, 13th to 15th Centuries

Franks: From Tribe to "Empire" 🛑

After the fall of the Roman Empire, which was due in part to invasions from Germanic tribes, those tribes settled throughout Western Europe. Most of the tribes converted to Christianity relatively quickly, though politically they continued to run their own shows. This meant that they came into regular conflict with one another, formed alliances, and expanded—sometimes enough to be considered kingdoms. The most significant of these early kingdoms was the **Franks**, founded by **King Clovis.**

Key People: King Clovis

- He united tribes under his leadership in the 5th century to create the Frankish kingdom.
- The kingdom stretched from modern-day Germany through Belgium into France. Paris was established as the capital.
- Clovis converted to Catholicism.
- After his death, his empire, which was divided among his sons, declined in importance.
- His leadership helped solidify much of Western Europe under a common culture.
    - This unity came in handy a couple centuries later when, in 732, Charles Martel led Frankish armies to stop the advancing Muslim armies in the Battle of Tours.

Clovis's Frankish descendants greatly expanded the kingdom's scope in terms of military might, geographical boundaries, and political influence:

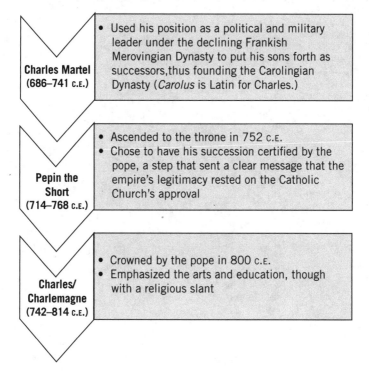

Charles Martel (686–741 c.e.)
- Used his position as a political and military leader under the declining Frankish Merovingian Dynasty to put his sons forth as successors, thus founding the Carolingian Dynasty (*Carolus* is Latin for Charles.)

Pepin the Short (714–768 c.e.)
- Ascended to the throne in 752 c.e.
- Chose to have his succession certified by the pope, a step that sent a clear message that the empire's legitimacy rested on the Catholic Church's approval

Charles/ Charlemagne (742–814 c.e.)
- Crowned by the pope in 800 c.e.
- Emphasized the arts and education, though with a religious slant

Charlemagne: The Empire Strikes Back ❗

In the centuries following the split of the Roman Empire, no true empire existed in Western Europe. The Franks had built a large kingdom, but it could hardly be considered an empire by historical standards. That changed with the coronation of **Charlemagne,** who began to centralize power despite the presence of the many kingdoms. Here are two key facts about his empire:

- The empire Charlemagne built would come to called the **Holy Roman Empire** in 962 C.E. (This had little to do with the original Roman Empire other than the fact that power was centralized again.)
- The Holy Roman Empire was much smaller than the original Roman Empire, comprising northern Italy, Germany, Belgium, and France.

The map below shows how the Frankish kingdom grew from Clovis's central European enclave into a superpower that unified much of the continent.

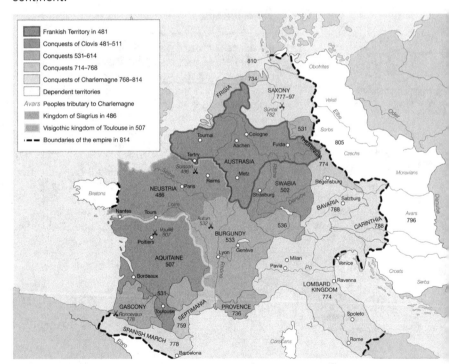

Central Europe c. 13th Century

The Holy Roman Empire did not last long at its peak size. Charlemagne had overall control of the empire, but the local lords held power over the local territories, answering to Charlemagne only on an as-needed basis. And because Charlemagne did not levy taxes, he failed to build a strong and united empire. After his death and the death of his son Louis, the empire was divided into thirds among his three grandsons according to the **Treaty of Verdun** in 843 C.E.

Vikings

During this time, Europe continued to be attacked by powerful invaders, notably the **Vikings,** who were perhaps the most successful of these invaders.

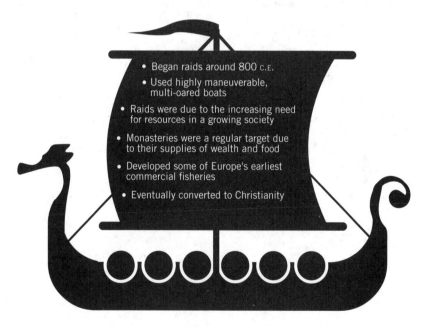

- Began raids around 800 C.E.
- Used highly maneuverable, multi-oared boats
- Raids were due to the increasing need for resources in a growing society
- Monasteries were a regular target due to their supplies of wealth and food
- Developed some of Europe's earliest commercial fisheries
- Eventually converted to Christianity

The Vikings weren't Europe's only terrorizers. The **Magyars** from Hungary also conducted raids in Western Europe.

The Medieval Church

One of the most significant actions taken by the medieval church was the **Crusades**. Pope Urban wanted

- Jerusalem, the most important city in Christianity, to be in the hands of Christians
- to find a common cause that would reunite the Roman Catholic Church and the Eastern Orthodox Church

He found the opportunity to achieve both of these goals in 1096 c.e.

CAUSE
- Muslims, in particular the Seljuk Turks, expanded into territories that Christians had historically associated with Christianity, including the Holy Land (present-day Israel and Palestine).

ACTION
- Pope Urban sent soldiers to the Holy Land.
- In 1204 c.e., a total of four crusades failed to produce any long-term results for the Christians despite occasional victories.

EFFECTS
- The eastern and western churches grew even further apart.
- Amid violence and uncertainty, most of the Holy Land remained in the hands of Muslim Arabs.
- The Crusades resulted in centuries of mistrust between Christians and Muslims.

Three Things to Know About the Crusades ❗

❶ The Crusades were motivated not only by religious beliefs, but also by political and economic incentives. The lure of empire and wealth was a major factor for many.

❷ Intentional religious expansionism can be just as devastating and powerful as politically driven military invasion. The death, rape, pillaging, and slavery perpetuated in the name of religion was startling.

❸ Failed efforts at conquest and expansion still have a major impact on world history. The Crusades led to interaction between cultures that otherwise might not have interacted, fueling trade and leading to Europe's discovery of its ancient past (which, you may recall, was preserved by Muslims). This rediscovery was key for Europe's Renaissance.

Ongoing contact with Muslims during the European Middle Ages (whether from the Crusades or otherwise) had the unintentional effect of leading many European Christians to question the central authority of the Church, as mapped out in the diagram below.

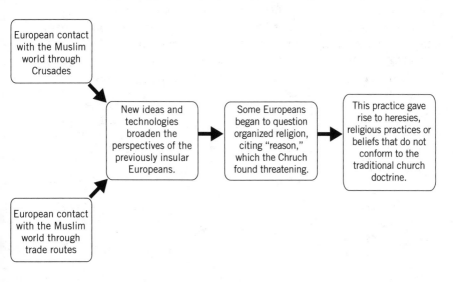

Doubts about the supremacy of religious dogma continued to emerge until the beginning of the 13th century, when **Pope Innocent III** issued strict decrees on church doctrine. A few years later, Pope Gregory IX set into motion the now notorious **Inquisition**.

Under Pope Innocent III... 💬	Under the Inquisition... ❗
• **Heretics** and Jews were frequently persecuted. • A fourth, ultimately unsuccessful, crusade was attempted.	• Heretics underwent formalized interrogation and persecution. • Punishment for so-called nonbelievers ranged from excommunication and exile to torture and execution.

> ⊜   Due to the pervasiveness of the church and its ultimate power at this time, it is sometimes referred to as the **Universal Church** or the **Church Militant**.

The Birth of Scholasticism 💬

The introduction of new thoughts and technologies into Europe weakened the supremacy of the Church by encouraging people to think more openly. One effect of this was the founding of universities, where men (not women) could study philosophy, law, and medicine and learn from the advances made in Muslim countries.

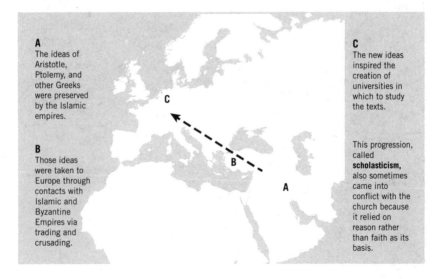

A
The ideas of Aristotle, Ptolemy, and other Greeks were preserved by the Islamic empires.

B
Those ideas were taken to Europe through contacts with Islamic and Byzantine Empires via trading and crusading.

C
The new ideas inspired the creation of universities in which to study the texts.

This progression, called **scholasticism,** also sometimes came into conflict with the church because it relied on reason rather than faith as its basis.

Late in the 13th century, **Thomas Aquinas** (1225–1274 c.e.), a famous Christian theologian of this period, made significant inroads in altering Christian thought. He wrote *Summa Theologica*, which outlined his view that faith and reason are not in conflict but rather gifts from God, and each can be used to enhance the other.

Black Death ❗

Cultural diffusion via trade resulted in the spread of religions, languages, art, and ideas. At times, it also resulted in the spread of disease and plague. The **Bubonic Plague** (also called the Black Death) started in Asia in the 14th century and was carried by merchants along the trade routes all the way to Europe.

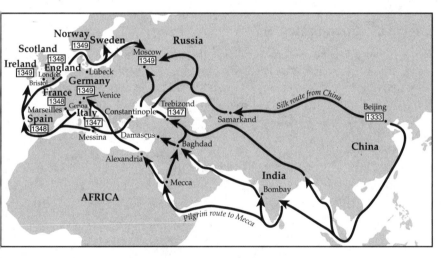

Spread of the Black Death, 1333–1349 c.e.

Causes of the Plague	Effects of the Plague
• Mongol control of the Asian silk routes increased the interaction between Europe and Asia. • Crowded conditions in Europe's cities and a lack of adequate sanitation and medical knowledge contributed to the plague's rapid spread.	• The plague destroyed entire communities and killed as many as one out of three people in Western Europe. • It quickened the decline of feudal society because many manors were not able to function.

The dramatic changes brought about by the epidemic—a shift toward a commercial economy, more individual freedom, and the development of new industries—sped up social and economic movements that were already impacting Europe.

Origins of Nation-States ❗

The European nations we are familiar with today did not pop up overnight. Rather, they involved a coming together of people with shared histories, identities, languages, and cultures (as well as some good old-fashioned conquest). The challenges and growing pains of three European nation-states are presented in the following table.

Nation	Origin	Challenge	Growth	Legacy
England	In 1066 c.e., **William the Conqueror**, a Norman (Viking), led an invasion during a power struggle. His victory began a tradition of a strong monarchy in England.	One of William's descendants, King John, had fallen out of favor with his nobles due to a combination of weak leadership, losing land to France, and being an all around horrible human.	In 1215 c.e., the nobles forced King John to sign the **Magna Carta**, a document that reinstated feudal rights to the nobles and extended the rule of law to others, namely the growing burgher class.	The Magna Carta laid the foundation for Parliament—the House of Lords (nobles and clergy) presided over legal issues and advised the king, while the House of Commons (knights and wealthy burghers) oversaw issues of trade and taxation.
France	In 987 c.e., **King Hugh Capet** ruled only a small area around Paris; for the next couple of hundred years, subsequent kings expanded this territory.	Beginning in the 12th century, England began to claim large parts of present-day France. By the early 15th century, England claimed the entire French territory.	As a teenager, **Joan of Arc**, a farm girl, claimed to have heard voices that told her to liberate France from the hands of the English. She somehow convinced French authorities to allow her to lead an army into battle. With her army, she forced the English to retreat from Orleans.	While she was eventually captured, tried by the English, and burned at the stake by the French, Joan of Arc had a significant impact on the **Hundred Years' War** (1337-1453) between England and France, which resulted in England's withdrawal from France.

Nation	Origin	Challenge	Growth	Legacy
Spain	**Queen Isabella**, ruler of the kingdom of Castile, married **Ferdinand**, heir to the Spanish kingdom of Aragon, in 1469 C.E. to unify Spain under a single monarchy.	Rather than compete with the Church for authority, Isabella and Ferdinand formed an alliance with the Catholic Church, effectively ending religious toleration in the region.	Newly unified and energized, Spain embarked on an imperial quest that led to tremendous wealth and glory, eventually resulting in the spread of the Spanish language, customs, and Christianity to much of the new world.	Non-Christians (predominantly Muslim and Jewish people) were forced to convert to Christianity or leave the country. This marked the beginning of the **Spanish Inquisition**, bringing about tragic consequences for non-Christian Spaniards.

❗ In Germany, the reigning family died without a successor to the emperorship, creating a period known as **interregnum** (a time between kings). Both Germany and Italy became decentralized in a group of strong, independent townships and kingdoms, similar to city-states. In this environment, merchants and tradespeople became more powerful (through groups such as the Hanseatic League, for example).

Medieval Russia ❗

In the 9th century, St. Cyril—an Orthodox Christian who used the Greek alphabet to create a Slavic alphabet—converted many of the Slavic peoples of southeastern Europe and Russia to Christianity.

In the late 10th century, **Vladimir**, a Russian prince from Kiev, sent envoys to study the world's religions, eventually landing on Orthodox Christianity for his country and abandoning the traditional pagan religion. Besides its religion, there were a number of other ways in which Russia differed culturally from Western Europe.

Russia	Western Europe
Russia spent over a century occupied by the Tatars, a group of Mongols who defeated Russia in 1242 c.e., and ruled a large chunk of the country.	Western Europe spent the Middle Ages rebuilding into kingdoms after the raids from Germanic tribes, which had resulted in the fall of Rome.
After Mongol power declined, the power of Russian princes grew. In fact, one such prince, Ivan III, declared himself **czar** (the Russian word for emperor or Caesar). By the mid-1500s, **Ivan the Terrible** consolidated power over the entire Russian sphere, ruling ruthlessly and using the secret police against his own nobles.	The power of royals began to decrease as nobles asserted themselves against their monarchs, and burghers used economic influence to gain a powerful foothold.

 Ask Yourself...

1. How did the relationship between religious institutions and political offices differ in Eastern and Western Europe?
2. How did the early challenges nation-states experienced ultimately solidify nationhood?

Developments in Asia

China

The three powerful Chinese dynasties during this period—**T'ang** (618–903 c.e.), **Song** (960–1279 c.e.), and **Ming** (1368–1644 c.e.)—experienced golden ages, each with its own unique characteristics. T'ang and Song are often grouped together (though they are very different), while the Ming came to power after a brief period of domination by Mongol invaders, a dynasty known as the **Yuan**.

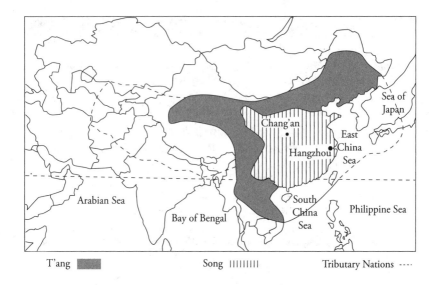

Extent of the T'ang (618–907 C.E.) and Song (960–1279 C.E.) Dynasties

Notable Chinese Emperors 💬

Emperor	Reign	Dynasty	Accomplishment
Wu Zhao	690–705 C.E.	T'ang	The first and only empress of China, Wu Zhao was both ruthless toward adversaries and compassionate toward peasants.
Xuan-zong	712–756 C.E.	T'ang	Xuan-zong expanded Chinese territory into parts of Manchuria, Mongolia, Tibet, and Korea. The enormous T'ang China eventually collapsed under its own weight, however.
Taizu	960–976 C.E.	Song	Taizu reunified China after the collapse of the T'ang Dynasty.

At the height of both the T'ang and Song dynasties, China was relatively stable.

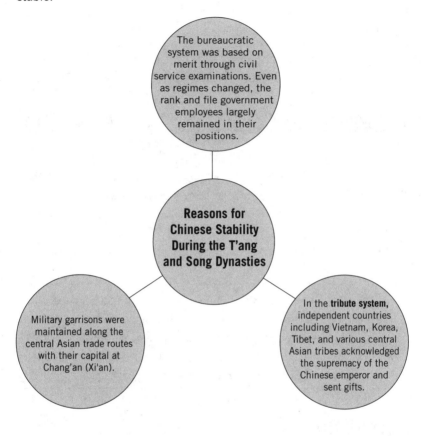

The bureaucratic system was based on merit through civil service examinations. Even as regimes changed, the rank and file government employees largely remained in their positions.

Reasons for Chinese Stability During the T'ang and Song Dynasties

Military garrisons were maintained along the central Asian trade routes with their capital at Chang'an (Xi'an).

In the **tribute system,** independent countries including Vietnam, Korea, Tibet, and various central Asian tribes acknowledged the supremacy of the Chinese emperor and sent gifts.

Despite the relative stability of the T'ang Dynasty, a large-scale peasant rebellion known as the **An Lushan Rebellion** severely weakened China during this dynasty. The An Lushan Rebellion was in a similar vein as the Nika riots in the Byzantine Empire, only this one lasted more than 7 years!

Chinese Culture ❗

If there is one characteristic of Chinese culture during this time period that stands out above all others, it is its innovation. From the 7th to the 13th centuries, the T'ang and then the Song made great strides in virtually every category of human endeavor: art, architecture, science, philosophy, porcelain-making, silk-weaving, construction of transportation systems, and more.

Innovations of the T'ang Dynasty	Innovations of the Song Dynasty
• Gunpowder	• Encyclopedias
• Magnetic clock	• Histories
• Poetry	• Junks (the best ships of the time)
• Porcelain	• Magnetic compass
	• Moveable type (brought literacy to the lower classes)
	• Paper money

~ One area in which this culture was not forward-thinking was gender roles and treatment of women. Foot-binding, a practice in which young girls' feet were tightly bound to prevent them from growing, was a widespread during this period—large feet were considered masculine and ugly. This practice resulted in severe physical deformities.

Religion in China 💬

Chang'an, a renowned trade center, was the world's most cosmopolitan city during this period. Characterized by a religiously diverse and multinational population, religious tolerance was practiced, though with some exceptions.

Following the fall of the Han Dynasty, a number of religions had influenced China:

- Buddhism
- Daoism
- Nestorianism
- Manicheaism
- Zoroastrianism
- Islam

The religion that arguably had the greatest impact was Buddhism, especially in its two forms: Mahayana and Chan (Zen in Japan). Mahayana had widespread appeal because of its emphasis on a peaceful and quiet existence separated from worldly values. Meanwhile, Chan Buddhism won converts among the educated classes, who generally followed Confucianism due to its focus on meditation and appreciation of beauty.

Reaction Against Buddhism in China 💬

- Daoists saw Buddhism as a rival religion that was winning over many of its adherents.
- In the mid-800s C.E., under Emperor Wuzong, a wave of persecutions destroyed thousands of monasteries and reduced the influence of Buddhism in China.
- Confucians saw Buddhism as a drain on both the treasury and the labor pool, especially because Buddhism dismissed the pursuit of material accumulation.

Neo-Confucianism in China 💬

- New ideas about Confucian philosophy arose in the late T'ang and early Song dynasties as China turned away from the worldly ideas of Buddhism.
- In contrast to the older Confucian focus on practical politics and morality, Neo-Confucianism borrowed Buddhist ideas about the individual.
- This approach became the basis of civil service with a systematic approach to both the heavens and the role of the individual.

Japan ❗

A group of islands off the coast of mainland Asia, Japan remained relatively isolated for thousands of years. While ideas, religions, and material goods traveled between Japan and the rest of Asia, especially China, the rate of cultural exchange was limited. In fact, little is known of early cultures in Japan prior to 400 C.E. except that they were influenced by Korea and China.

The Yamato Clan

The **Yamato** clan, Japan's first important ruling family, emerged as leaders in the 5th century C.E. and has remained the only dynasty to rule Japan.*

Brief Overview of Early Japanese History

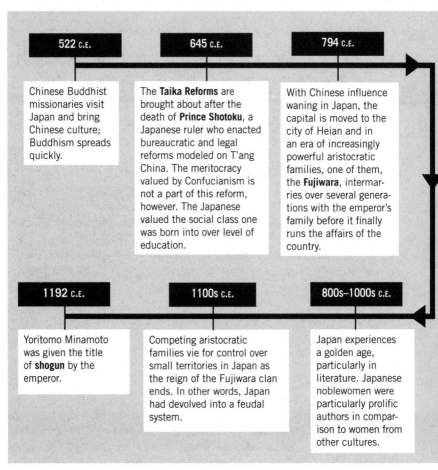

522 C.E.

Chinese Buddhist missionaries visit Japan and bring Chinese culture; Buddhism spreads quickly.

645 C.E.

The **Taika Reforms** are brought about after the death of **Prince Shotoku**, a Japanese ruler who enacted bureaucratic and legal reforms modeled on T'ang China. The meritocracy valued by Confucianism is not a part of this reform, however. The Japanese valued the social class one was born into over level of education.

794 C.E.

With Chinese influence waning in Japan, the capital is moved to the city of Heian and in an era of increasingly powerful aristocratic families, one of them, the **Fujiwara**, intermarries over several generations with the emperor's family before it finally runs the affairs of the country.

1192 C.E.

Yoritomo Minamoto was given the title of **shogun** by the emperor.

1100s C.E.

Competing aristocratic families vie for control over small territories in Japan as the reign of the Fujiwara clan ends. In other words, Japan had devolved into a feudal system.

800s–1000s C.E.

Japan experiences a golden age, particularly in literature. Japanese noblewomen were particularly prolific authors in comparison to women from other cultures.

Fun fact: The current emperor of Japan is a descendant of the Yamato clan. That's some serious staying power.

Feudal Japan ❶

The interesting thing about feudalism in Japan is that it developed around the same time as feudalism in Western Europe, but independently. Just like European feudalism, the socioeconomic hierarchy was bound together in a land-for-loyalty exchange.

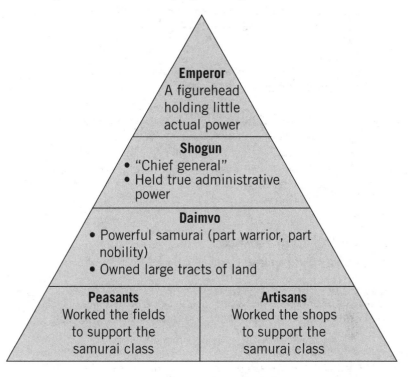

Emperor
A figurehead holding little actual power

Shogun
- "Chief general"
- Held true administrative power

Daimvo
- Powerful samurai (part warrior, part nobility)
- Owned large tracts of land

Peasants
Worked the fields to support the samurai class

Artisans
Worked the shops to support the samurai class

The samurai followed a strict code of conduct known as the **Code of Bushido**, which was very similar to the code of chivalry in Europe. The code stressed loyalty, courage, and honor—so much so that if a samurai failed to meet his obligations under the code, he was expected to commit suicide.

Religion in Japan

The **Shinto** religion took hold early on in Japan. When Buddhism arrived later, it did not replace Shinto. Instead, most Japanese people adopted Buddhism while also hanging on to their Shinto beliefs. In other words, they followed both religions simultaneously.

Key Facts About Shinto

- Shinto means "the way of the gods."
- The Japanese worshipped ***kami,*** which are spirits found in nature (the forces of nature) and in ancestors.
- The goal of Shinto is to become part of the *kami* by following certain rituals and customs.
- The Yamato clan claimed that the emperor was a direct descendant of the sun goddess, which helped the clan stay in power.

Compare and Contrast Them: European and Japanese Feudalism

Differences	Similarities
• In Europe, women were adored if they possessed feminine traits; in Japan, women lived harsher, more demeaning lives. • The feudal contract in Europe was a legally binding contract. In Japan, the arrangement was based solely on group identity and loyalty.	• Both systems were rooted in political structure, social structure, and an honor code. • Feudal arrangements in both systems were based on the culture. • Both systems persisted for a long time due to how entrenched in the cultures they were.

Japan Maintains Its Identity

Even though China had a significant impact on Japan, the Japanese people retained a strong cultural identity.

> **Key Differences Between Chinese and Japanese Cultures**
>
> - In Japan, birth, not education or other outside influences, was a more important indicator of social class and career opportunities.
> - Japan's aristocracy remained strong.
> - Japan continued to observe the rites of its indigenous religion, Shinto, despite the influences of Confucianism and Chan Buddhism.

Korea and Vietnam

Chinese armies had been in Korea and Vietnam as early as the Han Dynasty due to the leaders' desire to expand, whether via trade or by force. But it was the large-scale military campaigns of the T'ang that resulted in cultural exchanges in both regions. Korea and Vietnam each maintained a distinctive, complicated relationship with China. However, the Viet people were more skeptical of China than were the Koreans and therefore fought relentlessly to keep an independent culture. Regardless, both nations could not avoid the influence of Chinese culture. Take a look at the following table.

Korea	Vietnam
• Korea became a vassal-state of the T'ang to maintain cordial relations with the far more powerful Chinese. • Due to the tribute system, Korean schools and its imperial court were reorganized to mirror that of China. The power of the nobility in Korea prevented a true merit-based bureaucracy. • The tribute system also led to the introduction of Confucianism and Buddhism to Korea.	• The Viet people were unwilling to accept even the appearance of a tribute relationship with China, and actively resisted the T'ang armies. • A tribute relationship was eventually established, leading to Confucian schools in Vietnam and an active relationship between the two entities. However, the Viet continued to revolt against the T'ang. • The Vietnamese maintained their independence in the face of Chinese expansion, even after the fall of the T'ang.

In Vietnam, where rice is an essential crop requiring significant moisture, farmers developed a process known as **terracing**, which creates flat, step-like layers along hills. The purpose of terracing is to retain water and soil for the crops by preventing run-off and erosion. The technology was independently developed in North America, South America, Europe, and Central Asia as well.

India

India, the birthplace of two religions—Hinduism and Buddhism—saw the introduction of a new religion in the 10th century: Islam. Islamic invaders set up shop in Delhi under their leader, the sultan. The kingdom, known as the **Delhi Sultanate**, spread Islam for three centuries beginning in 1206. Under the Delhi Sultanate, colleges were created, irrigation systems were improved, and Hindu architects and artists oversaw the construction of mosques.

Not everything about this arrangement was friendly, however. Muslims in this theoretically tolerant regime taxed nonbelievers and even destroyed some Hindu temples. Many Hindus in northern India converted. Sometimes the conversions were genuine; other times, they just made life easier. In general, many Hindus in northern India converted to Islam, while those in southern India retained their Hindu traditions.

Contrast Them: Islam and Hinduism

Islam and Hinduism have often clashed. Here are some key differences:

Islam	Hinduism
Monotheistic	Polytheistic
Holds that all people are equal under God	Upholds the caste system
Cows = food	Cows = sacred
Sees itself as tolerant of other beliefs and even mixed with other beliefs	Sees itself as universal and exclusive

The Rise and Fall of the Mongols 🛈

The Mongols, the epitome of a nomadic culture, had existed for a long time as rival tribes and clans who remained fairly isolated from the rest of the world. In the early 1200s, however, all of that changed.

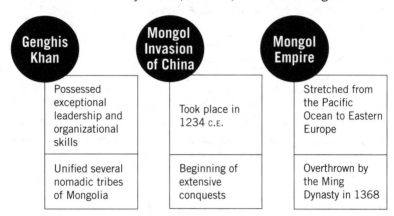

Genghis Khan	Mongol Invasion of China	Mongol Empire
Possessed exceptional leadership and organizational skills	Took place in 1234 c.e.	Stretched from the Pacific Ocean to Eastern Europe
Unified several nomadic tribes of Mongolia	Beginning of extensive conquests	Overthrown by the Ming Dynasty in 1368

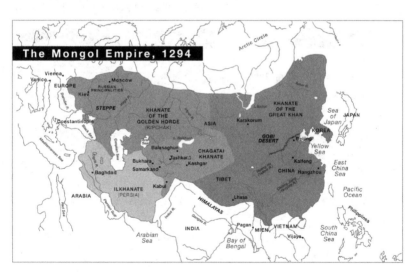

The Mongol Khanates

The Mongols weren't called ruthless warriors for nothing. They knew how to fight and were highly organized and mobile. The consequences of putting up a fight against Mongols meant certain destruction of the entire village, so most learned to not resist.

Decentralized Mongols 💬

The sheer size of the Mongol Empire ultimately proved to be too large to maintain centralized control. However, this did not stop the Mongols from doing what they did best: conquering.

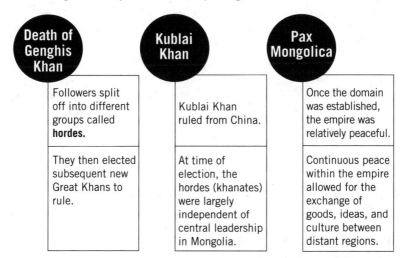

Death of Genghis Khan	Kublai Khan	Pax Mongolica
Followers split off into different groups called **hordes.**	Kublai Khan ruled from China.	Once the domain was established, the empire was relatively peaceful.
They then elected subsequent new Great Khans to rule.	At time of election, the hordes (khanates) were largely independent of central leadership in Mongolia.	Continuous peace within the empire allowed for the exchange of goods, ideas, and culture between distant regions.

Notable Hordes 💬	
Golden Horde	**Timurid Empire**
• Founded by Batu Khan in the 1240s • Located in a region of modern-day Russia • Treated Russia as a vassal state. As a consequence, Russia did not unify or culturally develop as quickly as its European neighbors to the west.	• Founded by **Timur Lang (Tamerlane),** who wanted to restore the empire of Genghis Khan • Stretched across Persia and parts of central Asia • Invaded India; Tamerlane's armies destroyed everything in sight and massacred thousands, and the sultanate was destroyed • Mongols eased up after Tamerlane returned to his capital in Central Asia (Samarkand); the sultanate was restored • Islam continued to grow in India (under Mongol control) over the next few centuries.

The Persistence of Chinese Culture Under the Mongols ❗

The Mongols turned out to be great diffusers of culture. Some Mongols assimilated into the cultures of the places they conquered. For instance, after the Mongols conquered Persia, most converted to Islam. Elsewhere, Mongol culture remained separate. When Mongols conquered China, for example, Kublai Khan dismissed Confucian scholars, forbade marriage between Mongols and the Chinese, and prohibited the Chinese people from learning the Mongol language.

Because the Chinese weren't allowed to **Mongolize**, they kept their own identity. In 1368, the Chinese kicked out the Mongols, ending the Yuan Dynasty. The Chinese then established the Ming Dynasty under traditional Chinese practices.

 The heyday of the Silk Road was back during the Han Dynasty, but its use was revived during the Mongol reign and experienced heavy traffic once again. The important thing to know about the Silk Road is that it carried so much more than silk; it also saw the transport of goods such as paper and porcelain, religion (Buddhism, Islam, Christianity), food products, and military technology. Perhaps more importantly, it was one of the most effective ways that the East and West interacted.

Ask Yourself...

1. What factors allowed innovation to flourish under the T'ang and Song dynasties?
2. To what extent did Japan maintain a culture unique from China?
3. What impact did the Mongols have on the different regions of Asia?

Developments in Africa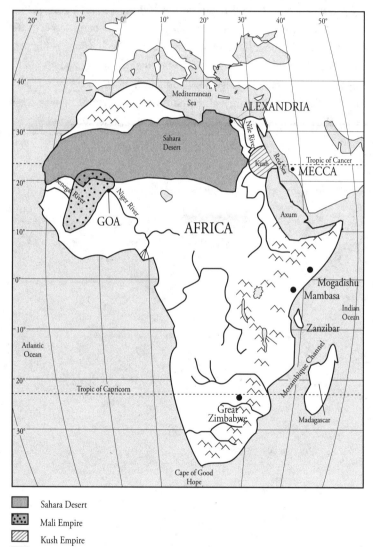

Some of the civilizations discussed in this section existed long before 600 C.E., but we've included them here so that you can study these key African civilizations as a group.

African Empires and Trade Cities

East Africa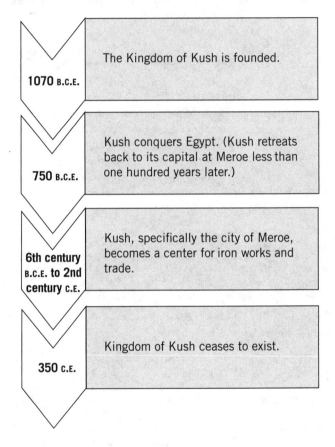

The **Kush** and **Axum** civilizations developed to the south of Egypt in the upper reaches of the Nile River.

Kush

1070 B.C.E.	The Kingdom of Kush is founded.
750 B.C.E.	Kush conquers Egypt. (Kush retreats back to its capital at Meroe less than one hundred years later.)
6th century B.C.E. to 2nd century C.E.	Kush, specifically the city of Meroe, becomes a center for iron works and trade.
350 C.E.	Kingdom of Kush ceases to exist.

Axum ⓘ

After the Kush went into decline around 200 C.E., another empire, **Axum**, rose to greatness to the south in modern-day Ethiopia.

	What to Know	Significance

Economy	• Its coastal location made it ideal for world trade.
	• Trade with overseas (and overland) Muslims began in the early 10th century.
	• Swahili traders brought the following to the coast for trade (among other items):
	  ○ gold
	  ○ slaves
	  ○ ivory
		• The incredible wealth generated by trade resulted in the growth of powerful kingdoms and trading cities along the coast in advantageous locations.
		• Like wealthy trading cities throughout the world, they became cultural and political centers.

Religion	• 4th century C.E.: The Axum Empire converted to Christianity. • 7th century C.E.: Many converted to Islam.	• It is clear that the Axum were in constant contact with the Mediterranean world. • To facilitate political and economic relationships, the ruling elites and merchant classes of the eastern African kingdoms converted to Islam, but maintained many of their own cultural traditions. Eventually, Islam spread throughout most of East Africa.

Culture	East African culture was influenced by the combination of two factors. The east coast of Africa was • linked to Arabia, Persia, India, and Southeast Asia through the shipping lanes of the Indian Ocean trade • populated by Bantu-speaking peoples who settled into lives of farmers, merchants, and fishermen	These influences created what is called **Swahili** culture. In fact, the whole area is called the Swahili coast, from the Arabic word for "coasters" or traders, and the Swahili language is a combination of Arabic and Bantu.

West Africa 🔟

Kush and Axum were located in eastern Africa, along the Nile River and near the Red Sea, giving them easy access to other cultures. The cultures of **Ghana, Mali,** and **Songhai,** however, were in West Africa, south of the Sahara, making their access to North African trade routes quite difficult.

Islamic Traders 🔟

West African traders initially traveled into the Sahara Desert in search of salt. As the Muslim Empire spread across North Africa in the 7th and 8th centuries, Islamic traders also penetrated the Sahara Desert to reach the fertile, wealthy interior of Africa. When West African traders encountered Islamic traders along the salt road, they started trading for a lot more than just salt—the West African kingdoms of Ghana (c. 800–1000 c.e.) and Mali (c. 1200–1450 c.e.) were sitting on tons of gold!

Constant trade brought more than just Islamic goods to Ghana and Mali; it brought Islam as well. For Ghana, the result was devastating. The empire was subjected to a Holy War led by an Islamic group intent on converting (or else killing) them. While Ghana defeated the forces, the empire ultimately fell into decline. By the time Mali came to power, however, the region had already converted to Islam in a more peaceful transition.

Impact of Islamic Traders in West Africa

- Ghana (c. 800–1000 c.e.)
  - An Islamic group intent on converting them waged a Holy War.
  - Ghana defeated the forces, but their empire fell into decline.
- Mali (c. 1200–1450 c.e.)
  - A peaceful transition followed as the region had already converted to Islam.

Key People: Mansa Musa

- Mali ruler
- Built a capital in Timbuktu
- Expanded the kingdom well beyond the borders of Ghana
- In 1324, made a notable pilgrimage to Mecca, complete with an entourage of hundreds of gold-carrying servants and camels

---

Songhai Empire ❗

The largest empire in West Africa, the **Songhai Empire,** formed in the mid-15th century when Sonni Ali conquered the region. **Timbuktu** became a major cultural center during the Songhai Empire, complete with a university that drew scholars from around the Islamic world.

Benin

Located near present-day Nigeria, artists from **Benin** mastered a bronze-sculpting technique. They made clay molds around a wax carving, melted the wax, filled the mold with melted bronze, and, after breaking the clay mold, revealed some of the most beautiful early bronze work created by any civilization.

Oral literature was an important part of life in most African communities. History and stories were passed from one generation to the next, not through written texts, but through storytelling.

Ask Yourself...

In what ways did interaction with Islam transform African cultures?

Developments in the Americas ❗

The three great civilizations that developed in what is now Central and South America are the **Maya,** the **Aztec,** and the **Inca.**

Early American Civilizations

Maya Decline: Where Did They Go? ❗

The Maya actually began during the time of the classical civilizations discussed in the previous chapter.

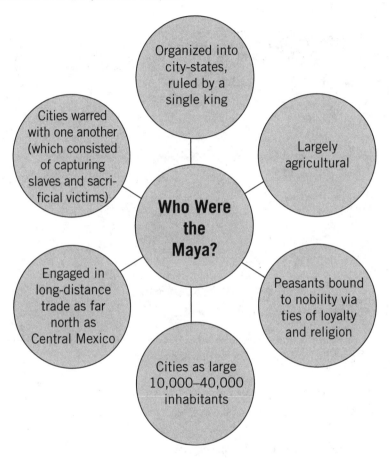

The decline of the Maya remains a source of debate. They began to abandon cities around 800 C.E.

Theories About Why Mayan Civilization Ended

1. Political dissention and social unrest
2. Natural disaster
3. Environmental degradation and overuse of land
4. Outside invaders

Aztecs ❗

The Aztecs, also known as the Mexica, arrived in central Mexico in the mid-1200s and built their capital at **Tenochtitlan** (modern-day Mexico City).

Aztec Civilization			
Government	**Military**	**Religion**	**Women's Roles**
• Empire was large but lacked a bureaucratic form of government. • Regions (even conquered ones) could self-govern as long as they paid tribute.	• Expansionist policy • Professional army • Warriors were an elite class in the social structure. • Through conquest and alliances, the Aztecs built an empire of up to 12 million people.	• Human sacrifice (victims obtained by the military) • 10,000s of men and women sacrificed annually, including for religious occasions such as the dedication of a new temple	• Subordinate public role; primarily charged with running the household • Could inherit property • Involved in skilled crafts, such as weaving and even commerce

Compare Them: The Aztec Civilization and the Roman Empire

Although the Aztecs and Romans developed large civilizations continents and centuries apart, they were similar in at least two respects:

• Built roads to connect their vast empires
• Allowed people they conquered to govern themselves, as long as they paid taxes (tribute)

Because of the improved transportation systems (roads) and the diversity of cultures under their control, both the Aztecs and the Romans were able to adapt ideas from the people they conquered and use them for their own purposes. The Aztecs and the Romans were conquerors as well as borrowers.

Incas 🛑

The Inca Empire, set in the Andes Mountains in Peru, was also expansionist in nature. At its zenith, it is thought to have controlled more than 2,000 miles of South American coastline. The capital at Cuzco may have had as many as 300,000 people in the late 1400s.

Incan Civilization				
Government	**Economy**	**Military**	**Religion**	**Women's Roles**
State bureaucracy manned by the nobility, which · controlled the empire by traveling on a complex system of roads	• Concept of private property did not exist; the ruler, descended from the sun, owned everything on Earth. • Incans had no large animals, so humans were the primary labor source.	Rulers felt the need to ensure their place in eternity by securing new land, which meant conquest.	• Polytheistic, though the sun god was at the center of the religion • Sacrificed material goods, animals, and occasionally humans	• Expected to work the fields, weave cloth, and care for the household • Could pass property to their daughters as well as take on religious roles

---

How Did They Do It?

The Incas controlled their territory with...
- a professional army
- an established bureaucracy
- a unified language
- a complex system of roads and tunnels

Building an Empire 💬

The Incas were excellent builders, stonecutters, and miners. Their skills are evident from the ruins of the **Temple of the Sun** in **Cusco** and the temples of **Machu Picchu**.

Trade in the Americas ❗

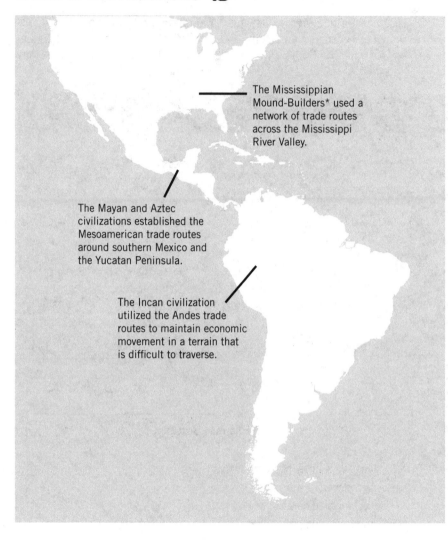

The Mississippian Mound-Builders* used a network of trade routes across the Mississippi River Valley.

The Mayan and Aztec civilizations established the Mesoamerican trade routes around southern Mexico and the Yucatan Peninsula.

The Incan civilization utilized the Andes trade routes to maintain economic movement in a terrain that is difficult to traverse.

 The who?! The Mound-Builders is the name given to a group of cultures that, over thousands of years, constructed earthen mounds for a variety of purposes, from religious to residential. You may not be asked about this group on the AP Exam, but keep it in your back pocket in case you're ever a contestant on *Jeopardy!* (or just shouting answers at your TV from home).

Agricultural Innovations 💬

South and Central America faced various agricultural challenges. The Maya, for instance, occupied poorly drained lowlands in Central America and adapted by building terraces to trap the silt drained by numerous rivers. Here are a couple of other examples of agricultural technology used in the Americas:

Technique	Region	Purpose
Chinampa field systems	Mexico	Grow crops on top of shallow water
Waru waru agricultural technique	South America	Raise crop beds to prevent erosion and control water distribution

 Ask Yourself...

Which characteristics did the Central American civilizations share with the Incan civilization? In what ways were they different?

Review of Interactions Among Cultures, c. 600 c.e.–1450 ❗

The purpose of this section is to help you pull together the events that occurred during this time period and view them from a global perspective. The following examples are just some of the ways that people interacted between c. 600 and 1450 c.e. We strongly suggest that you add your own examples based on what you've read in this book as well as in your AP World History class.

Trade Networks and Cultural Diffusion

The following trade networks and patterns developed during this time period:

- Mediterranean trade between Western Europe, the Byzantine Empire, and the Islamic Empire
- Hanseatic League
- Silk Road (used heavily from 1200–1600 c.e.)
- Land routes of the Mongols
- Trade between China and Japan
- Trade between India and Persia
- Trans-Saharan trade routes between West Africa and the Islamic Empire

---

Key Travelers During This Period

Xuanzang, a Chinese Buddhist monk, traveled throughout the T'ang Dynasty and into India to understand how Buddhism is practiced in different parts of Asia.

Marco Polo, a merchant from Venice, made his way to China and back to Europe.

Islamic traveler **Ibn Batutta** experienced unbelievable adventures (seriously, his travels are more interesting than any *Indiana Jones* movie) on his way through the Islamic world into India and China before returning to Africa.

Each of these travelers wrote extensively of their journeys. When people in their homeland read about their travels, they developed an understanding of cultures in other parts of the world. These three men also took elements of various cultures to their destination, performing a kind of one-man cultural diffusion.

Expansion of Religion and Empires: Culture Clash ❶

A major theme of this chapter is how empire expansion led to cultural interaction and the intentional diffusion of religions. By "intentional diffusion of religions" we mean methods such as missionary work or religious warfare as opposed to the natural spread of religious ideas that occurs when people come into contact with each other.

Examples of this include the following:

- Mongol expansion into Russia, Persia, India, and China
- Invasion of Germanic tribes into southern Europe and England
- The Vikings' expansion from Scandinavia into England and Western Europe
- The Magyars' push into Western Europe
- The Islamic Empire's expansion into Spain, India, and Africa
- The Crusades
- Buddhist missionaries in Japan
- Orthodox Christian missionaries in Eastern Europe

Other Reasons People Were on the Move ❗

Interaction among and within civilizations occurred during this time period for many reasons other than trade or conquest:

Growing Populations
- Germanic tribes moved into southern Europe.
- More people in cities = opportunities in the cities = people move away from the countryside.

Lure of Large Cities
- People were attracted to capitals, which would at times move to create the impression of a large empire (e.g., Abbasids and Baghdad).
- Universities were built, drawing people from around an empire.

Pilgrimages
- Rome and Constantinople attracted pilgrims to their great cathedrals.
- The Islamic duty to travel to Mecca was the most significant religious pilgrimage in terms of scale and cultural representation.

In each of these examples, people who did not live together in the past were now living together. The result? More cultural diffusion.

Technology and Innovations, c. 600 C.E.–1450 !

The cultural interaction that occurred during this period spurred new ideas and innovations. Much of this innovation came from eastern societies, such as China and India, and were then filtered through the Islamic world. By 1450, most of these new ideas had made their way to Europe, following the Crusaders, merchants, and missionaries. The following table lists items introduced to Europeans by both Muslims and the Chinese.

Islamic World	China
paper mills (from China)	gunpowder cannons
universities	moveable type
astrolabe and sextant	paper currency
algebra (from Greece)	porcelain
chess (from India)	terrace farming
modern soap formula	water-powered mills
guns and cannons (from China)	cotton sails
mechanical pendulum clock	water clock
distilled alcohol	magnetic compass

This time period also saw groups around the world develop new technologies in accordance with their knowledge of the environment. The mastery of these technologies allowed civilizations to master skills ranging from conquering to raiding to trading.

Listed below are some examples of technological adaptations that drew from environmental knowledge:

- **Vikings**—Use of longboats for trading and raiding
- **Arabs and Berbers**—Use of camels to efficiently traverse and establish trade with African cultures
- **Mongols**—Use of horses to conquer villages and move swiftly across large areas of land

Changes and Continuities in the Role of Women ❗

The spread of Islam, the openness of Christianity and Buddhism, the development of new empires based on wealth and acquisition of property, and the revitalization of neo-Confucianism impacted the status of women around the world.

Women's Status in Medieval Societies			
Europe	**Islamic Societies**	**India**	**China**
Strict patriarchal social divisions	Equality in religion, but separate in mosque	Strict patriarchal caste system	Strict Confucian social order and guidelines for virtuous behavior
Could inherit land and take oaths of vassalage, but property belonged to husband	Received half the inheritance of male children	Child marriages	Had access to dowries and owned businesses
Could bring court cases but not participate in the decision	Testimony had less weight than that of men	Practice of *sati* for widows (practice of committing suicide after husband's death)	Widow to remain with son; no property if remarried
Division of labor; women in textiles	Allowed to hold roles ranging from farming to textiles	Family textile labor	Silk weaving as female occupation
Christian monogamy	Concubines and seclusion in harems	Marriage limited to caste members	Concubines and seclusion in harems

Women's Status in Medieval Societies			
Europe	**Islamic Societies**	**India**	**China**
Education limited to upper class males	Literate society	Education limited	Literate society, but state education limited to men
Did not recognize children born outside of marriage	All children, even those born out of marriage, seen as legitimate	Common to have children outside of marriage (no stigma)	Fairly common to have children outside of marriage. These children were usually raised by the father's family and eligible for inheritance.
Veiling of upper class	Veiling in public	*Purdah*: veiling or seclusion	Foot binding

Women in Africa ❗

Trade and the arrival of new religions did not significantly change the role of women in African societies.

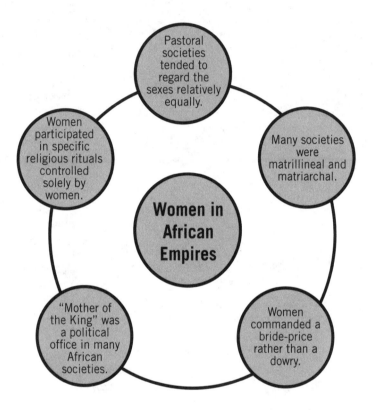

Pastoral societies tended to regard the sexes relatively equally.

Many societies were matrilineal and matriarchal.

Women participated in specific religious rituals controlled solely by women.

Women in African Empires

"Mother of the King" was a political office in many African societies.

Women commanded a bride-price rather than a dowry.

Although both Islam and Christianity found converts in Africa, women were less eager to convert than men and the practice of veiling was met with mixed reactions.

Ask Yourself...

1. Did some cultures benefit more from the trade routes than others? How?
2. Would all of the technologies developed during this period have been created even without cultural diffusion? Which ones were dependent on interactions?

Timeline of Major Developments, c. 600 C.E. – 1450 🛑

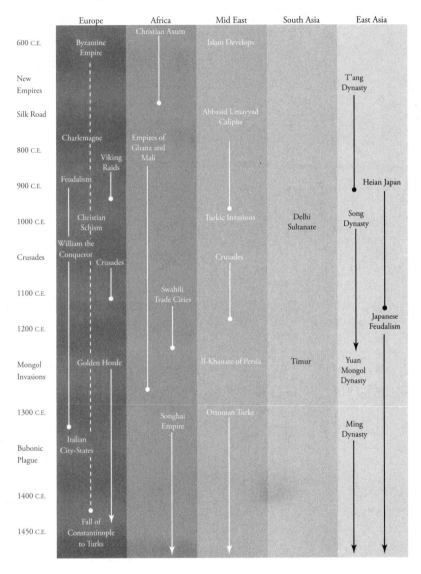

	Europe	Africa	Mid East	South Asia	East Asia
		Christian Axum			
600 C.E.	Byzantine Empire		Islam Develops		
New Empires					T'ang Dynasty
Silk Road			Abbasid Umayyad Caliphs		
800 C.E.	Charlemagne	Empires of Ghana and Mali			
		Viking Raids			
900 C.E.	Feudalism				Heian Japan
1000 C.E.	Christian Schism		Turkic Invasions	Delhi Sultanate	Song Dynasty
Crusades	William the Conqueror		Crusades		
		Crusades			
1100 C.E.		Swahili Trade Cities			
1200 C.E.					Japanese Feudalism
Mongol Invasions	Golden Horde		Il-Khanate of Persia	Timur	Yuan Mongol Dynasty
1300 C.E.		Songhai Empire	Ottoman Turks		Ming Dynasty
Bubonic Plague	Italian City-States				
1400 C.E.					
1450 C.E.	Fall of Constantinople to Turks				

PERIOD 4

c. 1450 to c. 1750

Cultures became even more connected during this Age of Exploration, which was put into motion by the need to trade goods and a desire to build empires. While African and many Asian empires used technologies of the new global trade networks to expand, Far Eastern civilizations sought isolation from the Western World. Meanwhile, religious, artistic, scientific, and intellectual revolutions in Europe promoted new ways of looking at the world during this time period.

Global Interactions, c. 1450 to c. 1750

Period 4, c. 1450 to c. 1750, is the time period when world history truly becomes *world* history. This era is known as the "early modern" period to distinguish it from the "medieval" period that preceded it and from the "modern" industrial world whose foundations it laid.

Here are some key things that happened during this time period:

- The Eastern and Western Hemispheres became permanently connected to each other, and European nations came to dominate many regions of the world.

- Using new technologies of sea travel and navigation, European explorers brought their languages, governments, and religions to the Americas. They also brought millions of slaves from Africa, along with the European diseases that would decimate Native American populations.

- Around the world, trade networks expanded and governments began to build massive empires of colonies and trading posts all over the world.

This chapter is organized into two sections. The first section is about the major revolutions of Europe from 1450 to 1750, including the Renaissance, Reformation, Enlightenment, and Scientific Revolution. The second section is a region-by-region survey of the world during this period.

The revolutions discussed in this chapter did not develop completely independent of one another. The Renaissance was deeply tied to traditional religion, as was the Scientific Revolution. Sir Isaac Newton was a devout Christian who saw almost no contradiction between his scientific discoveries and his theological beliefs. At the same time, new scientific discoveries led people to question traditional dogmas of the Catholic Church and the literal truth of the Bible.

The Artistic Revolution: The Renaissance ❶

The **Renaissance** is one of the most important revolutions that marked the end of the Middle Ages in Europe. The word *renaissance* literally means "rebirth." In this case, it refers to the rebirth of arts, philosophy, and literature that began in Italy in the 14th century and spread to the rest of Europe. Renaissance writers and artists consciously revived the wisdom of ancient Greek and Roman writers and applied it to their Christian worldview.

Art ❶

The work of Leonardo da Vinci, Michelangelo, and other Italian painters and sculptors differed from medieval art in its realistic depiction of human bodies and the influence of classical art and themes.

Humanism ❶

Humanism was an intellectual movement emphasizing human concerns over the divine or supernatural, and was a move away from medieval Christian ideology. It was influenced by ancient Greek and Roman texts.

Literature ❶

Writers began to experiment with new literary forms and to revive stories and characters from the ancient world. Instead of writing in traditional Latin, they began to write in vernacular, or spoken, languages, such as German, French, and English. At the same time, Johannes Gutenberg's printing press allowed for the circulation of texts far and wide.

William Shakespeare and the English Renaissance

During the 16th century, English artists and writers flourished even as political
and religious changes transformed English society.
William Shakespeare wrote his influential plays during the reign of
Queen Elizabeth. Like other Renaissance authors, he wrote in the vernacular
(English), discussed nonreligious themes, and focused on the
condition of real human beings.

 Ask Yourself...

1. What are the differences between the art of the Middle Ages and the
   Renaissance?
2. How can art be used as a primary source for a major philosophical
   change?

The Religious Revolution: The Protestant Reformation

Another revolution that marked the end of the Middle Ages was the religious revolution known as the **Protestant Reformation.** Medieval Europe was dominated by the Catholic Church, and there were few outlets for religious belief and practice outside the Church. That changed around the year 1500 when theologians like **Martin Luther** and **John Calvin** challenged many of the teachings and traditions of the Catholic Church.

The Protestant Critique	The Catholic Response
• Martin Luther led the charge against what he saw as excesses in the Catholic Church. According to the popular legend, Luther nailed a copy of his 95 Theses to the door of the Wittenberg Castle church.* • Luther denounced the sale of indulgences, blessings of forgiveness in exchange for money or goods, which he claimed were used to exploit and control people. • Luther and the other reformers believed that the Bible should be translated from Latin into vernacular languages so that everyone could read and interpret the text for themselves. • Protestants promoted the idea that salvation occurred by faith alone rather than by good works.	• The Catholic Church responded to the Protestant Reformation by punishing Protestant dissent and by passing positive reforms. • At the **Council of Trent** (1545–1563), Catholic leaders denounced Protestant theology as heretical, or contrary to Christian teaching. • Catholic leaders insisted that salvation occurred by a combination of faith and good works.

The Jesuits

Ignatius Loyola founded the Society of Jesus in 1540. Members of the society came to be known as the Jesuits. They created a new Catholic intellectual culture and spread Catholicism around the world.

 Martin Luther set out to change the relationship between the Church and its people. You might say he *nailed it!*

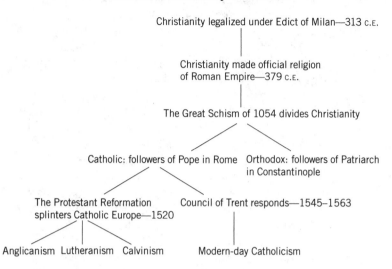

Evolution of Christianity: A Timeline

Christianity legalized under Edict of Milan—313 C.E.

Christianity made official religion
of Roman Empire—379 C.E.

The Great Schism of 1054 divides Christianity

Catholic: followers of Pope in Rome   Orthodox: followers of Patriarch
in Constantinople

The Protestant Reformation   Council of Trent responds—1545–1563
splinters Catholic Europe—1520

Anglicanism Lutheranism Calvinism   Modern-day Catholicism

Christianity Goes Global ❗

The Protestant Reformation and Catholic Counter-Reformation changed the course of world history. If Europeans had never gained dominance in seafaring, trade, and exploration, the Reformation may have remained a local religious dispute in Western Europe. As it was, Europeans conquered the globe in the 16th century and their religious dispute became a worldwide export.

King Henry VIII and the Church of England

The mission of spreading Christianity became a century-long war between the European countries beginning with King Henry VIII. He was so anxious about having a male heir that he broke ties with the Catholic Church and started the Protestant Church of England in order to divorce his first wife. Other Catholic countries such as Spain later used this move toward Protestantism as a reason for war.

The Protestant Missionaries

Protestants were particularly preoccupied with spreading the Gospel, or good news of salvation by faith in Jesus Christ. England became a Protestant nation under **Henry VIII** in 1534, so future English colonies, such as the American colonies, would be primarily Protestant.

The Catholic Missionaries

Catholic leaders took the threat of Protestantism very seriously and dispatched Jesuits to work as missionaries in the New World and Asia. Crucially, the world's first global empire was built by the Spanish, who were staunch Catholics and enabled the diffusion of Catholicism all over North and South America.

The turmoil of the Protestant Reformation also had a political effect. Many monarchs were closely tied to the Catholic Church and relied on the blessing of the Pope as justification to rule. This **divine right** reasoned that God chose them to rule without a responsibility to a higher power. It is different from the Chinese **Mandate of Heaven** by which emperors were allowed to stay in power only if they were acting in line with the will of the heavens.

The pressures of the Protestant Reformation become a threat to the monarch's "divine right to rule," and many, such as Henry VIII and Louis XIV, broke with the Catholic Church claiming "absolute rule."

Intellectual Revolutions in Science and Philosophy

In the period from around 1550 to 1700, the **Age of Reason** transformed Europe into a modern continent and marked the beginnings of modern science, philosophy, and politics. Two important developments occurred during the Age of Reason: the **Scientific Revolution** and the **Enlightenment.**

The Scientific Revolution: Quick Facts

- The Scientific Revolution began when **Nicolaus Copernicus** argued for a heliocentric (sun-centered) solar system.
- Scientists such as **Galileo** and **Sir Isaac Newton** began to tinker with new tools such as telescopes and developed the **scientific method** based on empirical principles.
- Scientists focused on what can be known from logic, evidence, reason, and experimentation. Some of their findings put them in direct conflict with traditional religion.

The Enlightenment: Quick Facts

- The Enlightenment celebrated scientific knowledge and reason.
- The emphasis on science and reason challenged the traditions of the monarchy and the Catholic Church. For example, Enlightenment thinking rejected the "divine right" of monarchs to rule absolutely over their subjects.
- Theorists **John Locke** and **Jean-Jacques Rousseau** developed the theory of the **social contract,** which claimed that rulers have power only if their subjects consent to it.
- Many Enlightenment thinkers were **deists** who believed that God did not actively intervene in the natural world.

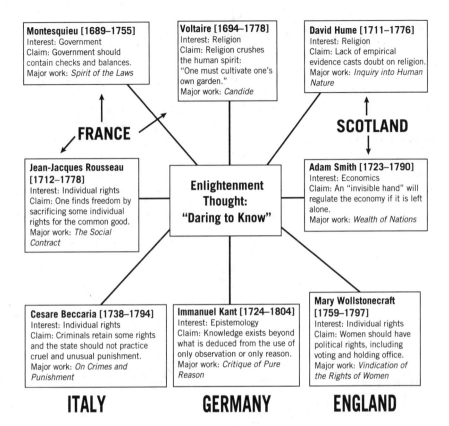

Montesquieu [1689–1755]
Interest: Government
Claim: Government should contain checks and balances.
Major work: *Spirit of the Laws*

Voltaire [1694–1778]
Interest: Religion
Claim: Religion crushes the human spirit: "One must cultivate one's own garden."
Major work: *Candide*

David Hume [1711–1776]
Interest: Religion
Claim: Lack of empirical evidence casts doubt on religion.
Major work: *Inquiry into Human Nature*

FRANCE

SCOTLAND

Jean-Jacques Rousseau [1712–1778]
Interest: Individual rights
Claim: One finds freedom by sacrificing some individual rights for the common good.
Major work: *The Social Contract*

Enlightenment Thought: "Daring to Know"

Adam Smith [1723–1790]
Interest: Economics
Claim: An "invisible hand" will regulate the economy if it is left alone.
Major work: *Wealth of Nations*

Cesare Beccaria [1738–1794]
Interest: Individual rights
Claim: Criminals retain some rights and the state should not practice cruel and unusual punishment.
Major work: *On Crimes and Punishment*

Immanuel Kant [1724–1804]
Interest: Epistemology
Claim: Knowledge exists beyond what is deduced from the use of only observation or only reason.
Major work: *Critique of Pure Reason*

Mary Wollstonecraft [1759–1797]
Interest: Individual rights
Claim: Women should have political rights, including voting and holding office.
Major work: *Vindication of the Rights of Women*

ITALY   **GERMANY**   **ENGLAND**

The Navigation Revolution

During the early modern period, Europeans developed new technologies in shipbuilding and navigation that enabled them to discover new lands, establish colonies and trading posts, and spread Christianity as a global religion. Many of these innovations built upon discoveries from the Asian and Islamic worlds. The image below highlights a few advances in navigation.

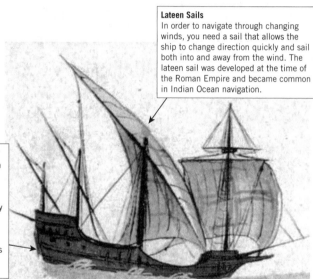

Lateen Sails
In order to navigate through changing winds, you need a sail that allows the ship to change direction quickly and sail both into and away from the wind. The lateen sail was developed at the time of the Roman Empire and became common in Indian Ocean navigation.

The Sternpost Rudder
To steer a ship, you need a rudder in the back of the ship. This invention came from the Chinese Han Dynasty and worked its way to Europe. These rudders were indispensable for the explorers in navigating along coastlines and across the difficult waters of the Atlantic Ocean.

Astrolabe
Before Google Maps or GPS systems, people had to find their way by using the sun and stars. The astrolabe was invented around the year 150 B.C.E. in the eastern Mediterranean and was popular throughout the Middle Ages.

Magnetic Compass
A ship captain must know his direction (north, south, east, west). The magnetic compass was invented by the Han Dynasty and adopted by European explorers.

Three types of ships fueled global exploration: the caravel, the carrack, and the fluyt*.

Caravel	• Portuguese sailing ship used to navigate the Atlantic Ocean and the western coast of Africa • Lightweight and effective for navigating into the wind, which gave the Portuguese a major advantage in the contest of building political and commercial outposts in Africa and the Indian Ocean	
Carrack	• Also known as a Nau ship • Had three or four masts • Able to carry enough cargo for long journeys, which enabled transatlantic voyages such as Christopher Columbus's discovery of the New World in 1492 and Magellan's circumnavigation of the world in the early 1500s	
Fluyt	• A large ship designed expressly for the purpose of carrying cargo • Developed in the Netherlands • Did not have heavy military defenses and could therefore travel more lightly and efficiently, which gave Dutch traders a huge advantage in the race to establish global trading corporations	

These ships were a far cry from the ocean liners and cruise ships that travel the world today. Any travelogue from this time period will tell you that sailing was treacherous and conditions on the ship were unpleasant (to say the least), not to mention unsanitary. Plus, pirates were a real threat!

Iberia Goes Global ❗

The first European nations to succeed in global exploration were Spain and Portugal. Both countries are located on the **Iberian Peninsula,** which is an ideal starting point for Atlantic and African travel. The Spanish and Portuguese had a long history of trading in both the Mediterranean Sea and the Atlantic Ocean and were eager to find a route to the markets of Asia. Spain and Portugal brought their languages to the New World, along with their Catholic religion, monarchical government, and distinct artistic and architectural styles.

Spain ❗

Spanish monarchs Ferdinand and Isabella funded the Italian explorer **Christopher Columbus** in his mission to find a way to the Indies. Columbus made four journeys eastward across the Atlantic Ocean, but they were all failures because Columbus never found his way to Asia. Instead, he made the most important discovery in the history of the world and brought the Americas under the control of European powers.

Portugal ❗

In his 1497 voyage, the Portuguese explorer **Vasco da Gama** became the first European to reach India by sea. He sailed all the way from Portugal along the coast of Africa, and then around the Cape of Good Hope to eastern Africa and India. The Portuguese set up ports along the coast of Africa and in Indian cities like Goa and Calicut and were a major political and economic power of the early modern period.

A few decades later, the Portuguese explorer **Magellan** became famous for circumnavigating the entire globe by ship from 1519 to 1522. It was a dangerous, complicated route, and Magellan died before it could be completed.

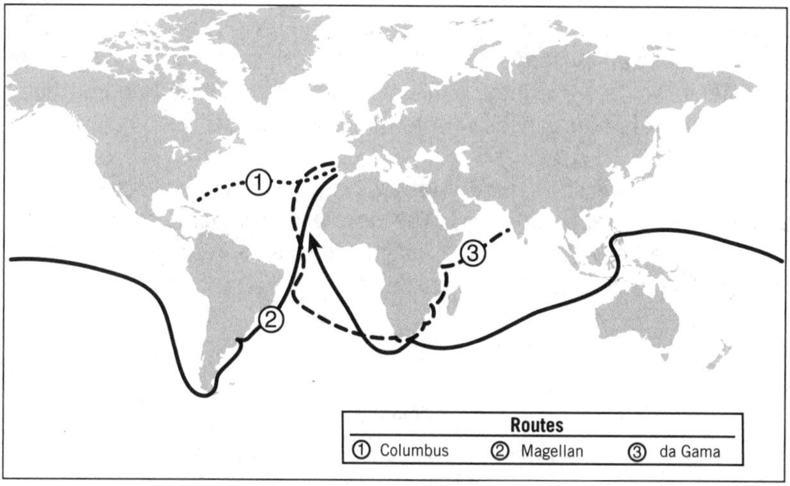

European Exploration in the Early 16th Century

Treaty of Tordesillas

Both Spain and Portugal claimed territories in the New World. To settle tensions between them, they signed the **Treaty of Tordesillas** in 1494, which divided the territory so that modern-day Brazil would be under Portuguese control, and the rest of the territory would go to Spain.

The Conquistadores

The Spanish did not just discover the New World; they conquered it and established the first transatlantic empire in world history. The Spanish conquest occurred on two fronts: in modern Mexico, where **Hernan Cortes** overthrew the Aztecs, and in modern Peru, where **Francisco Pizarro** overthrew the Inca. Cortes and Pizarro have become known as ***conquistadores*** (conquerors), which reminds us of the military nature of their takeover of the Americas.

The creation of "New Spain" in the Americas came at tremendous cost to the indigenous Native Americans. The diseases brought by the Europeans decimated local populations. Some scholars estimate that as much as 90 percent of the population was wiped out from disease alone. In addition, the Spanish launched military attacks and enslaved local populations into forced labor on farms. Finally, the Spanish established their legal system and Catholic religion, and, by extension, the **Inquisition,** which sometimes punished those who followed non-Catholic religious beliefs or practices with torture and even death.

Spanish society in the New World was organized by a strict social hierarchy based on race and class. The *encomienda* **system** of forced labor was organized around individual estates known as *haciendas,* in which the Spanish managed slaves and servants.

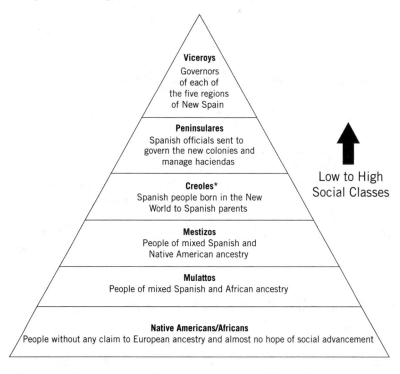

Viceroys
Governors
of each of
the five regions
of New Spain

Peninsulares
Spanish officials sent to
govern the new colonies and
manage haciendas

Creoles*
Spanish people born in the New
World to Spanish parents

Mestizos
People of mixed Spanish and
Native American ancestry

Mulattos
People of mixed Spanish and African ancestry

Native Americans/Africans
People without any claim to European ancestry and almost no hope of social advancement

Low to High
Social Classes

The creoles were caught in the middle of the complex hierarchy of the New World. Because they were not born in Spain, they were looked down on by the Spanish elite. Nevertheless, they were of European descent, so they were able to acquire education and wealth. The descendants of the early creoles eventually launched independence movements in the 18th and 19th centuries that led to the demise of the Spanish Empire.

The Commercial Revolution

The discovery of the New World opened up a whole new ocean for global commerce. The Atlantic Ocean was filled with exciting possibilities of acquiring new land, riches, plantations, and goods. It wasn't just governments that got in on the action—new businesses called **joint-stock ventures** allowed shareholders to own small pieces of trading companies that were setting up business in the New World. The most famous of these companies was the **Dutch East India Company**, which became established all over the world, especially in the Indian Ocean. This period also marked the beginning of the world's first global corporations.

The Columbian Exchange

The exchange of people, technology, ideas, and even diseases across the Atlantic Ocean was known as the **Columbian Exchange,** named after Christopher Columbus, who initiated the entire process by establishing transatlantic contact in 1492. This was the first time that goods such as tomatoes, corn, vanilla, and tobacco were introduced to Europeans and the first time that sugar, grapes, cattle, and wheat were introduced to the New World.

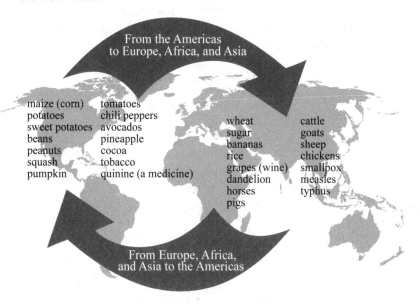

From the Americas
to Europe, Africa, and Asia

maize (corn)   tomatoes
potatoes   chili peppers
sweet potatoes avocados   wheat   cattle
beans   pineapple   sugar   goats
peanuts   cocoa   bananas   sheep
squash   tobacco   rice   chickens
pumpkin   quinine (a medicine) grapes (wine) smallpox
                                dandelion   measles
                                horses   typhus
                                pigs

From Europe, Africa,
and Asia to the Americas

The Columbian Exchange

Middle Passage

The **Middle Passage** refers to the shipment of African slaves across the Atlantic Ocean in the early modern period. Many ships originally left from Europe to Africa with goods to trade for slaves. Once the slaves were boarded in Africa, where they were packed in closely for maximum profit, they were taken to the New World to be traded or sold for goods headed to Europe. For them the journey was brutal, and millions of slaves died in the weeks-long voyage across the Atlantic Ocean.

Developments in Specific Countries and Empires, 1450–1750 ❗

Major movements like the Renaissance, Enlightenment, Scientific Revolution, Protestant Reformation, and Age of Exploration impacted different parts of Europe at different times, and the consequences of these developments varied by region. These movements drastically and permanently affected countries outside of Europe as well due to the growing global trade and territory expansion. The following timelines highlight the key dates during this time period and show how these developments played out for each European power.

Spain and Portugal ❗

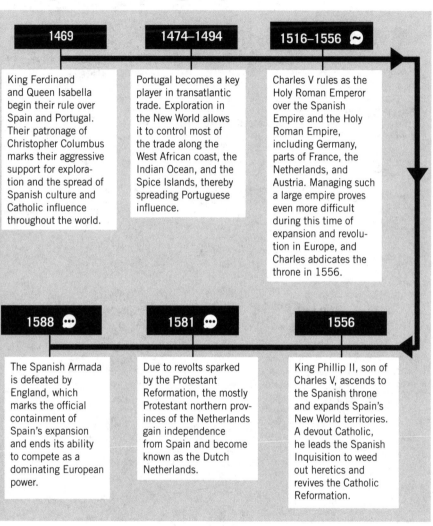

1469

King Ferdinand and Queen Isabella begin their rule over Spain and Portugal. Their patronage of Christopher Columbus marks their aggressive support for exploration and the spread of Spanish culture and Catholic influence throughout the world.

1474–1494

Portugal becomes a key player in transatlantic trade. Exploration in the New World allows it to control most of the trade along the West African coast, the Indian Ocean, and the Spice Islands, thereby spreading Portuguese influence.

1516–1556 💬

Charles V rules as the Holy Roman Emperor over the Spanish Empire and the Holy Roman Empire, including Germany, parts of France, the Netherlands, and Austria. Managing such a large empire proves even more difficult during this time of expansion and revolution in Europe, and Charles abdicates the throne in 1556.

1588 💬

The Spanish Armada is defeated by England, which marks the official containment of Spain's expansion and ends its ability to compete as a dominating European power.

1581 💬

Due to revolts sparked by the Protestant Reformation, the mostly Protestant northern provinces of the Netherlands gain independence from Spain and become known as the Dutch Netherlands.

1556

King Phillip II, son of Charles V, ascends to the Spanish throne and expands Spain's New World territories. A devout Catholic, he leads the Spanish Inquisition to weed out heretics and revives the Catholic Reformation.

 Remember!

You do not need to memorize the dates on these timelines, but you should be familiar with the chronology of events. Focus on the themes, patterns, and cause-and-effect relationships among these historical developments.

England ❗

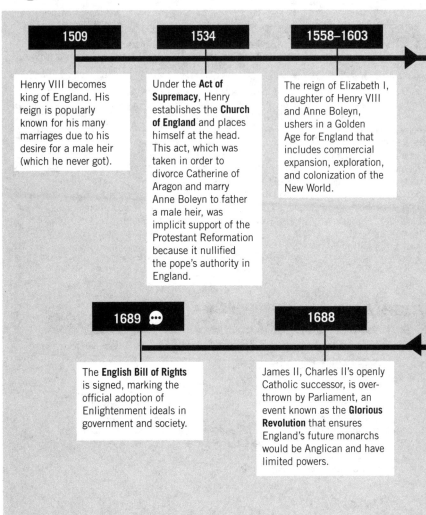

1509

Henry VIII becomes king of England. His reign is popularly known for his many marriages due to his desire for a male heir (which he never got).

1534

Under the **Act of Supremacy**, Henry establishes the **Church of England** and places himself at the head. This act, which was taken in order to divorce Catherine of Aragon and marry Anne Boleyn to father a male heir, was implicit support of the Protestant Reformation because it nullified the pope's authority in England.

1558–1603

The reign of Elizabeth I, daughter of Henry VIII and Anne Boleyn, ushers in a Golden Age for England that includes commercial expansion, exploration, and colonization of the New World.

1689 💬

The **English Bill of Rights** is signed, marking the official adoption of Enlightenment ideals in government and society.

1688

James II, Charles II's openly Catholic successor, is overthrown by Parliament, an event known as the **Glorious Revolution** that ensures England's future monarchs would be Anglican and have limited powers.

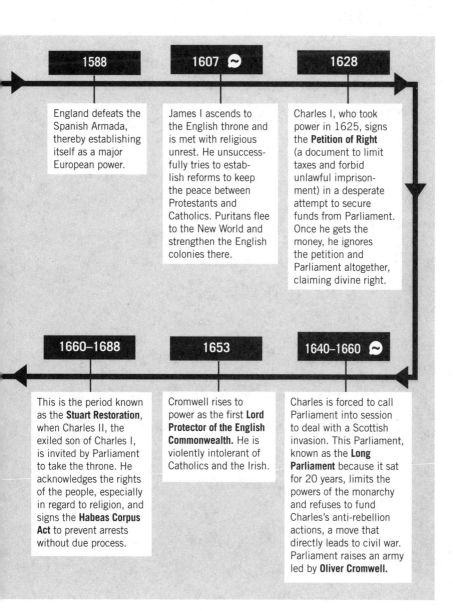

1588

England defeats the Spanish Armada, thereby establishing itself as a major European power.

1607

James I ascends to the English throne and is met with religious unrest. He unsuccessfully tries to establish reforms to keep the peace between Protestants and Catholics. Puritans flee to the New World and strengthen the English colonies there.

1628

Charles I, who took power in 1625, signs the **Petition of Right** (a document to limit taxes and forbid unlawful imprisonment) in a desperate attempt to secure funds from Parliament. Once he gets the money, he ignores the petition and Parliament altogether, claiming divine right.

1660–1688

This is the period known as the **Stuart Restoration**, when Charles II, the exiled son of Charles I, is invited by Parliament to take the throne. He acknowledges the rights of the people, especially in regard to religion, and signs the **Habeas Corpus Act** to prevent arrests without due process.

1653

Cromwell rises to power as the first **Lord Protector of the English Commonwealth.** He is violently intolerant of Catholics and the Irish.

1640–1660

Charles is forced to call Parliament into session to deal with a Scottish invasion. This Parliament, known as the **Long Parliament** because it sat for 20 years, limits the powers of the monarchy and refuses to fund Charles's anti-rebellion actions, a move that directly leads to civil war. Parliament raises an army led by **Oliver Cromwell.**

France ⚠

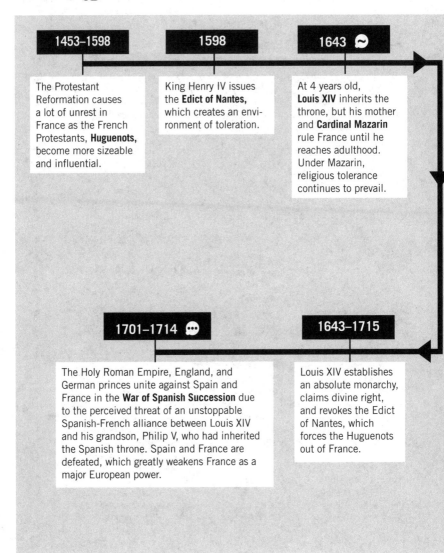

1453–1598

The Protestant Reformation causes a lot of unrest in France as the French Protestants, **Huguenots,** become more sizeable and influential.

1598

King Henry IV issues the **Edict of Nantes,** which creates an environment of toleration.

1643 🗨

At 4 years old, **Louis XIV** inherits the throne, but his mother and **Cardinal Mazarin** rule France until he reaches adulthood. Under Mazarin, religious tolerance continues to prevail.

1701–1714 💬

The Holy Roman Empire, England, and German princes unite against Spain and France in the **War of Spanish Succession** due to the perceived threat of an unstoppable Spanish-French alliance between Louis XIV and his grandson, Philip V, who had inherited the Spanish throne. Spain and France are defeated, which greatly weakens France as a major European power.

1643–1715

Louis XIV establishes an absolute monarchy, claims divine right, and revokes the Edict of Nantes, which forces the Huguenots out of France.

German Areas ❗

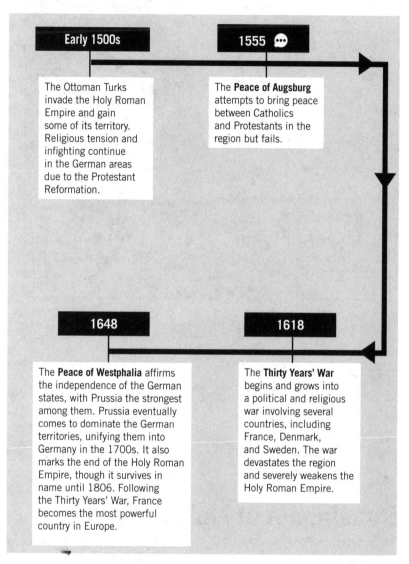

Early 1500s

The Ottoman Turks invade the Holy Roman Empire and gain some of its territory. Religious tension and infighting continue in the German areas due to the Protestant Reformation.

1555 💬

The **Peace of Augsburg** attempts to bring peace between Catholics and Protestants in the region but fails.

1648

The **Peace of Westphalia** affirms the independence of the German states, with Prussia the strongest among them. Prussia eventually comes to dominate the German territories, unifying them into Germany in the 1700s. It also marks the end of the Holy Roman Empire, though it survives in name until 1806. Following the Thirty Years' War, France becomes the most powerful country in Europe.

1618

The **Thirty Years' War** begins and grows into a political and religious war involving several countries, including France, Denmark, and Sweden. The war devastates the region and severely weakens the Holy Roman Empire.

By 1600, religious divisions across Europe looked like this:

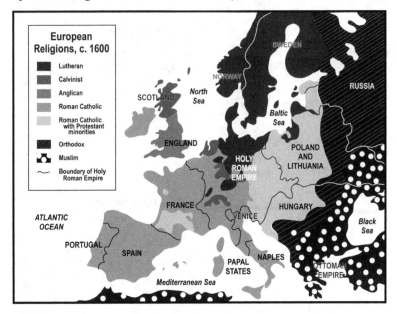

Religious Divisions c. 1600

 Ask Yourself...

1. How do European reactions to the Protestant Reformation and Enlightenment differ?
2. How successful is each country in expanding its territory?
3. Do you think conflict between the European powers was inevitable?

Russia: Out of Isolation

While Western Europe basked in the glow of the Renaissance, explored and expanded its influence across oceans, and debated about religion, science, and government in a series of movements, Russia remained isolated from the West and pushed eastward instead. During the 15th and 16th centuries and most of the 17th century, Russia did not experience any movement that could be labeled a Renaissance or Enlightenment; its growth was territorial, not intellectual or artistic.

It wasn't part of the Renaissance because it was under the control of the Mongols at the time. It wasn't part of the Reformation because it wasn't part of the Catholic Church in the first place. It wasn't until the late 17th century that Russia turned its eyes westward. Its history progressed along a very different path.

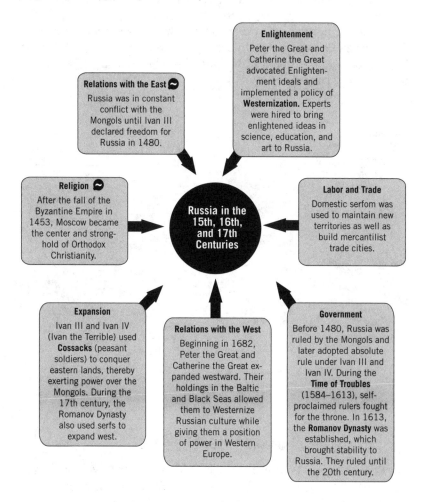

Enlightenment
Peter the Great and Catherine the Great advocated Enlightenment ideals and implemented a policy of **Westernization.** Experts were hired to bring enlightened ideas in science, education, and art to Russia.

Relations with the East 〰
Russia was in constant conflict with the Mongols until Ivan III declared freedom for Russia in 1480.

Religion 〰
After the fall of the Byzantine Empire in 1453, Moscow became the center and stronghold of Orthodox Christianity.

Russia in the 15th, 16th, and 17th Centuries

Labor and Trade
Domestic serfom was used to maintain new territories as well as build mercantilist trade cities.

Expansion
Ivan III and Ivan IV (Ivan the Terrible) used **Cossacks** (peasant soldiers) to conquer eastern lands, thereby exerting power over the Mongols. During the 17th century, the Romanov Dynasty also used serfs to expand west.

Relations with the West
Beginning in 1682, Peter the Great and Catherine the Great expanded westward. Their holdings in the Baltic and Black Seas allowed them to Westernize Russian culture while giving them a position of power in Western Europe.

Government
Before 1480, Russia was ruled by the Mongols and later adopted absolute rule under Ivan III and Ivan IV. During the **Time of Troubles** (1584–1613), self-proclaimed rulers fought for the throne. In 1613, the **Romanov Dynasty** was established, which brought stability to Russia. They ruled until the 20th century.

? Ask Yourself...

How does Russia's interactions during this period help set it up to become a major world power in the late 19th and 20th centuries?

Expansion of Islam in the Ottoman, Safavid, and Mughal Empires ❗

Three Islamic Empires rose nearly concurrently, conquering large swaths of land. Due to the organized use of artillery such as cannons and firearms, these empires were known collectively as the **Gunpowder Empires.** The **Ottoman Empire** covered much of the Middle East, Southeastern Europe, and Northern Africa, the **Safavid Empire** dominated Persia, and the **Mughal Empire** rose in India.

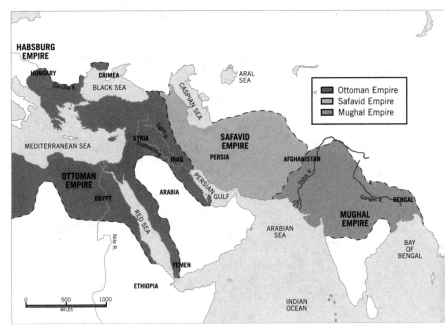

The Ottoman Empire (1299–1922) ❗

- **Constantinople → Istanbul**—In 1453, Constantinople was renamed Istanbul by the Ottoman Empire, led by **Osman Bey.** Istanbul became the center of Islam and religious tolerance.
- **Selim I**—He came to power in 1512 and expanded the Ottoman Empire, conquering the rest of the Byzantine Empire.
- **Suleiman I (the Magnificent)**—He ruled the Ottoman Empire from 1520 to 1566, ushering in a golden age. Suleiman I tried to conquer Europe but got only as far as Vienna. During his reign, the empire invested heavily in the arts and saw the greatest spread of Islam.

The Safavid Empire (1501–1722) 😐

- **Chief rivals**—Located in what is now Iran, the Safavids were the main rivals and eastern neighbors of the Ottoman Empire.
- **Islamic state**—The Safavid state was based on military conquest and dominated by Shia Islam.
- **Geography**—Its position between the Ottoman and Mughal Empires resulted in constant conflicts between the Muslim states, alliances with European nations against the Ottomans, and a continuation of the long-standing rift between the Sunni and Shia sects.

The Mughal Empire (1526–1857) 😐

- **Babur**—In 1526, Babur established the Mughal Empire, which came to dominate India for the next 300 years.
- **Religious tolerance**—The empire was tolerant of all religions, which allowed it to expand and unite India's northern and southern territories.
- **Akbar**—Ruling from 1556 to 1605, Akbar eliminated the *jizya**, encouraged religious tolerance and the arts, and raised the position of women in society.
- **Shah Jahan**—The **Taj Mahal,** which became a symbol of the Mughal golden age, was built during his reign.
- **England**—The empire was very active in trade with England, setting the stage for the colonization of India in the 1700s.

Jizya was a head tax on Hindus in the Islamic Mughal Empire. Hindus could practice openly but were additionally taxed for the privilege.

African Connections to the World 🔟

Beginning in the 10th century, strong centralized states formed in Africa due to the wealth accumulated from trade. Three major kingdoms were established—the **Songhai, Kongo,** and **Angola**—and their interactions with Europe and the Islamic world resulted in prosperity for Africa for a period of time in the 16th and 17th centuries. The following charts highlight the connections between these African kingdoms and other parts of the world.

Songhai Empire ➡	Trade with Islamic World ➡	Cultural Effects
• Empire built on conquests and military force • Ruled by **Sunni Ali** in the late 15th century, who consolidated territory along the Niger River Valley, as well as built a strong imperial navy and central government	• Used trans-Saharan trade for salt and gold from the Ottoman Empire	• Became an Islamic state • Grew prosperous and built Timbuktu as an Islamic center in Africa • Fell to the Moroccans, who had gunfire technology • Region south of the Songhai became the **Ashanti Empire,** which stretched along the West African coast, thriving due to the gold trade and its use of gunpowder

Kongo Empire →	Trade with Portugal →	Cultural Effects
• Empire on the northwestern coast of Africa • Strong centralized government	• Developed close economic and political ties with Portugal • Main export was slaves	• King **Alfonso I** converted to Catholicism; as a result, Kongo became a large Catholic influence in Africa. • The empire gained economic wealth and a circle of influence, with Portugal as an ally. • However, Portugal's growing desire for slaves led them to undermine the king's authority, and the Kongo Empire declined.

Angola Empire →	Trade with Portugal →	Cultural Effects
• Empire with access and trade routes into the interior of Africa • Ruled by **Queen Nzinga**	• Portugal set up a trading post in Angola as early as 1575 for the sole purpose of expanding its slave trade in Africa.	• Angola became extremely wealthy and influential in Africa, exerting control over the continent. • Portugal became increasingly demanding and domineering, leading to a 40-year war led by the warrior queen. Angola eventually lost, largely due to the superior weaponry of the Portuguese.

Asia and Imperialism ❗

China ❗

China was fortunate to have more stable leadership during this period, and their location also left them relatively isolated from European expansion. However, Chinese policies regarding exploration, trade, religion, society, and governance varied greatly between the two main dynasties. Use the following charts to identify the main causes for these shifts in policy.

	Ming Dynasty (1368–1644)	Qing Dynasty (1644–1911)
Exploration and Expansion	• Won China's independence from Mongolia in 1368 ☻ • **Zheng He,** a Chinese navigator, led China's exploration and expeditions, reaching East Africa before the Europeans. • Abruptly stopped exploration in the mid-15th century 💬	• Emperor **Kangxi** conquered Taiwan and expanded into Mongolia, central Asia, and Tibet. 💬 • Emperor **Qianlong** conquered Vietnam, Burma, and Nepal. 💬
Economy and Currency	• Constantly failing economy 💬 • Transitioned from paper currency to silver currency ☻	• Economically prosperous due to trade with Europe and territory expansion 💬

	Ming Dynasty (1368–1644)	Qing Dynasty (1644–1911)
International Trade	• Traded with Spain in the Philippines • Portugal established Macau for greater access to Chinese markets. • China suffered from constant pirating, causing them to shy away from trading internationally.	• Allowed trade rights to the Portuguese, Dutch, and British, but had absolute control over trade agreements • Often expelled European trade if there was a threat to Chinese culture • Restricted trade to only one city, Canton, in 1757 • Traded largely in tea, silk, and porcelain in exchange for silver
Culture and Society	• Centralized government with civil service exams ◐ • Isolationist society that allowed them to preserve and stabilize the country • Rejuvenation of traditional Chinese culture to solidify independence from Mongolian culture and influence	• Supported traditional Chinese arts • Continued civil service exams • The Ming were ethnically Manchu and oppressed ethnic Chinese in order to maintain their elite status, forbidding Chinese from learning the Manchu language, for example.
Religion	• Confucianism	• Strongly Confucian ⚫ • Banned Christianity in 1724

	Ming Dynasty (1368–1644)	Qing Dynasty (1644–1911)
Government and Politics	• Strongly isolationist • Dynasty based on Chinese ancestry and the right to rule	• Qing warriors, originally from Manchuria, had helped the Ming Dynasty defeat peasant rebellions, and then overthrew the Dynasty. • Manchu people remained the elite governing class and held all top-level positions in government. ✧ • Expanded trade and territories, but remained isolationist in policies

Japan ❗

During the 16th century, Japan was ruled by a series of **shoguns** while the emperor remained a figurehead. As time went on, power became more centralized at the same time that Japan was exposed to the West. In 1542, Portugal established trade with Japan, introducing guns and later Christian missionaries to the country. The Jesuits took control of the port city of Nagasaki, which put Japan well on its way to Westernization.

The move toward Westernization was reversed in 1600, however, with the birth of the **Tokugawa Shogunate,** also known as the **Edo Period,** by Tokugawa Ieyasu. This period ushered in a shift in attitudes toward the West, characterized by persecution of Christians and the **National Seclusion Policy** (1635), which closed Japan off to foreign influences as well as forbid the Japanese people to travel abroad.

Japan's isolationism led to a renaissance of Japanese culture. This renaissance saw the emergence of new art forms like **haiku** poetry and **kabuki** theater.

The following chart traces Japan's shift from Westernization to isolationism.

Shogun-Ruled Japan

Mid-1500s–1600
- Emperor was a figurehead and feudal lords controlled government.
- 1542—Portuguese established a trade agreement, causing Christian missionaries to stream into Japan and spread Christianity.

Tokugawa Shogunate and Edo Period

1600–1868
- The shogunate established a strict government that consolidated power away from the emperor and created a caste system.
- This period marked complete reversal in attitude toward the West.
- Christians were persecuted.
- In 1635, the **National Seclusion Policy** prohibited travel outside of Japan.

The Japanese Renaissance

1600–1868
- Isolationism brought about a time of great prosperity and cultural affluence.
- Kabuki theater and the haiku were created to exhibit Japanese culture.
- This period was similar to the European Renaissance in that the arts flourished.

Technology and Innovations, c. 1450–1750 ❶

The Age of Exploration opened the doors to cultural exchange as well as conflict. It also required new technology and innovations in weaponry, navigation, and communication to enable the European empires to become world powers.

Navigation ❶

Innovations in navigation allowed explorers to discover new continents and better trade routes, allowing Europeans to travel to these continents and expand their territories. This also enabled them to control overseas trade between Europe, Africa, Asia, and the New World.

Shipbuilding ❶

Advances in shipbuilding technology created bigger and better vessels that could travel across vast oceans. This allowed Europe to explore and conquer empires on other continents. Better ships also allowed for longer trade routes, which were essential for the African slave trade, and led to European imperial power and influence.

Weaponry ❶

The discovery of gunpowder in Asia led to innovations in weaponry. With rifles and cannons, Europeans were able to expand their territories more quickly and easily.

Printing Press ❶

The invention of the printing press by **Johannes Guttenberg** around 1440 revolutionized cultural exchange and enabled the spread of ideas across cultures and continents. This allowed empires like Spain and England to control and influence their territories from a distance. It also perpetuated the spread of Protestantism during and after the Reformation.

Ask Yourself...

1. How did Europeans use new technology to advance exploration at the expense of other countries and cultures?
2. How did the Europeans' use of new technology threaten their own power in relation to other European empires?
3. How did these innovations spread Enlightenment and Renaissance ideas and undermine the power of kings?

Changes and Continuities in the Role of Women ❗

There were many powerful female rulers during this time period, including Elizabeth I of England and Nur Jahan of Mughal India. Still, the status of women in general remained mostly unchanged. While the day-to-day lives of women improved with the introduction of products like textiles and spices, women were still considered property and inferior to men, who continued to be the holders of power and opportunity.

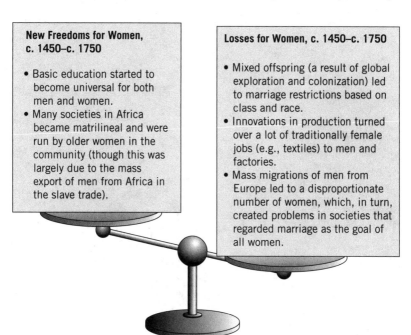

New Freedoms for Women, c. 1450–c. 1750

- Basic education started to become universal for both men and women.
- Many societies in Africa became matrilineal and were run by older women in the community (though this was largely due to the mass export of men from Africa in the slave trade).

Losses for Women, c. 1450–c. 1750

- Mixed offspring (a result of global exploration and colonization) led to marriage restrictions based on class and race.
- Innovations in production turned over a lot of traditionally female jobs (e.g., textiles) to men and factories.
- Mass migrations of men from Europe led to a disproportionate number of women, which, in turn, created problems in societies that regarded marriage as the goal of all women.

Ask Yourself...

1. What ideas or philosophies of this era are still influential today?
2. How did new technology pave the way for future developments?
3. Is there anything that could have prevented a European stronghold on global expansion?
4. What are the major events that make this a turning point in history for the world?

This period of exploration and global interaction led to the mixing and dilution of cultures as well as clashes between religions and policies. World powers were introduced during this time period, and the race to gain more intellectual, social, economic, and political power became a race to the top. This set the precedent for all future global interactions and conflict, which we'll explore in the next chapters.

PERIOD 5

c. 1750 to
c. 1900

This period is characterized by revolutions, both political and indus-trial. The fallout from many of these movements was a renewed sense of nationalism that played out on the world stage in the form of imperialism.

Industrialization and Global Integration, c. 1750 to c. 1900

Although this chapter covers only about 150 years, the world changed dramatically during this time period:

- Europe's influence waned in the West but rose in the East.
- Napoleon tried to conquer Europe.
- Italy and Germany became modern nation-states.
- Japan became an imperial power.
- The Industrial Revolution changed the world.

Enlightenment Revolutions in the Americas and Europe

As Enlightenment ideas began to spread throughout Europe, monarchical power started to subside. As people were sent out to fight in expansionist wars and taxed to pay for the new territory developments, Enlightenment ideas became an outlet for societal frustrations. By the late 1700s, concepts of individual rights, diverse and broad governments, and capitalism grew and eventually sparked revolutionary movements throughout the world. Perhaps the two most prominent revolutions that set the example for the rest of the world (especially the Spanish colonies) were the **American Revolution** and the **French Revolution.**

The American Revolution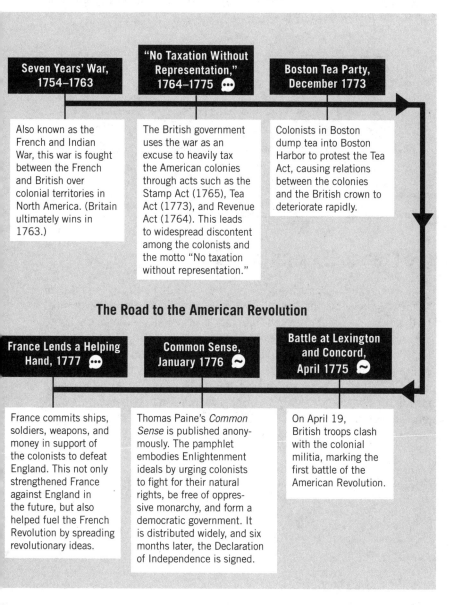

Seven Years' War, 1754–1763

Also known as the French and Indian War, this war is fought between the French and British over colonial territories in North America. (Britain ultimately wins in 1763.)

"No Taxation Without Representation," 1764–1775 💬

The British government uses the war as an excuse to heavily tax the American colonies through acts such as the Stamp Act (1765), Tea Act (1773), and Revenue Act (1764). This leads to widespread discontent among the colonists and the motto "No taxation without representation."

Boston Tea Party, December 1773

Colonists in Boston dump tea into Boston Harbor to protest the Tea Act, causing relations between the colonies and the British crown to deteriorate rapidly.

The Road to the American Revolution

France Lends a Helping Hand, 1777 💬

France commits ships, soldiers, weapons, and money in support of the colonists to defeat England. This not only strengthened France against England in the future, but also helped fuel the French Revolution by spreading revolutionary ideas.

Common Sense, January 1776 💬

Thomas Paine's *Common Sense* is published anonymously. The pamphlet embodies Enlightenment ideals by urging colonists to fight for their natural rights, be free of oppressive monarchy, and form a democratic government. It is distributed widely, and six months later, the Declaration of Independence is signed.

Battle at Lexington and Concord, April 1775 💬

On April 19, British troops clash with the colonial militia, marking the first battle of the American Revolution.

In 1781, French and American troops and ships cornered the British army and forced them to surrender. Within a decade, the Constitution and Bill of Rights were written, ratified, and put into effect.

💬 Causes and Consequences of the American Revolution

You don't need to know the details of the American Revolution for the AP World History Exam, but you should understand the impact of the Enlightenment as well as the mercantilist policies that led to discontent in the colonies. These forces—Enlightenment ideals and frustration over economic exploitation—are common themes in the world's revolutionary cries against colonialism throughout the 1800s.

The French Revolution ❗

France was involved in three wars in the 18th century: the **War of Spanish Succession,** the **Seven Years' War,** and the **American Revolution.** By the end of the century, the country's war debts were through the roof. Adding to this problem were drought and unbridled spending by King Louis XIV and the nobility, which created serious money problems for France. The king would need to raise taxes (which, of course, would not go over well). Moreover, during this time revolutionary ideas were brewing in France, thanks to the Enlightenment and American Revolution. Change was coming.

 If you've ever seen *Les Miserables* or heard the expression "Let them eat cake," you may already be a little bit familiar with the French Revolution.

The Estates General → The National Assembly → The Convention → The Directory ❶

Within just a few years, France underwent drastic governmental change. This change can be divided into three key phases, which are listed below. Before we get into that, however, it will help to know how French social classes, or estates, were structured:

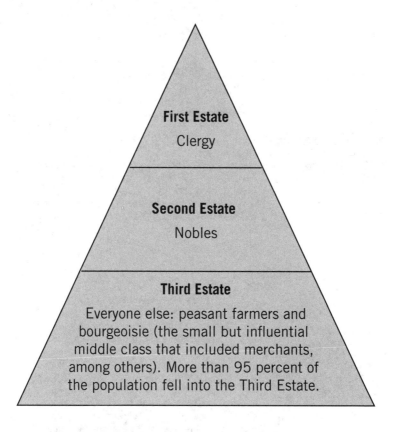

Note that 95 percent of the population belonged to the Third Estate. This is important in understanding the political events that occurred in France during this period.

Estates General

- The Estates General was called to session by Louis XIV in 1789 after having not met in about 175 years. (This body had been historically seen as unnecessary, as the king ruled by divine right.)
- It was comprised of representatives of the three estates of French society.
- The Third Estate wanted greater freedoms and suggested the Estates General meet as a unified body—all estates under one roof. They were overruled by parlement, which ordered the estates meet separately.

National Assembly

- June 17, 1789—Angered by parlement's decision and the sense they were being shut out by the other two estates, the Third Estate declared themselves the **National Assembly.**
- July 14, 1789—Peasants stormed the Bastille, a huge prison in Paris, inciting anarchy across the country- side.
- August 1789—The National Assembly adopted the **Declaration of the Rights of Man,** a document recognizing natural rights (and based on the American Declaration of Independence). Two years later, the National Assembly ratified a new constitution that established France as a constitutional monarchy—the king held on to executive power.

The Convention

- Unrest in France continued, as many had wanted to abolish the monarchy altogether.
- A new constitution was drawn up, and the **Convention** became the new ruling body. The Convention was headed by **Jacobins,** radicals who then executed the king and imprisoned the royal family.
- The Convention created the Committee of Public Safety, led by Maximilien Robespierre, to enforce revolutionary ideals. This ushered in the Reign of Terror during which tens of thousands of French citizens suspected of treason were beheaded. The French grew tired of Robespierre and beheaded him two years later.
- In 1795, a new constitution established the **Directory,** a five-man government.

Napoleon Bonaparte

An immensely popular and successful military star, Napoleon used his reputation to overthrow the Directory in 1799. He declared himself the First Consul under the new constitution. (If you're counting, that makes four constitutions since the Revolution began.)

Highlights from Napoleon's Reign

- **1789–1813**—Napoleon expanded French territory significantly and initiated many reforms in agriculture, infrastructure, and education.
- **1804**—His **Napoleonic Codes** recognized the equality of French (male) citizens and institutionalized some of the Enlightenment ideals that had sparked revolution in the first place.
- **1813**—Napoleon was defeated at Waterloo by a European coalition headed by **Prince von Metternich** of Austria, **Alexander I** of Russia, and the British **Duke of Wellington,** who had united against a common threat.
- **1815**—Napoleon was sent into exile, and the alliance met about what to do about France and its territories. This meeting was known as the **Congress of Vienna.**

Congress of Vienna (1815) ❗

The Congress decreed that a **balance of power** should be maintained among the existing powers of Europe in order to avoid the rise of another Napoleon.

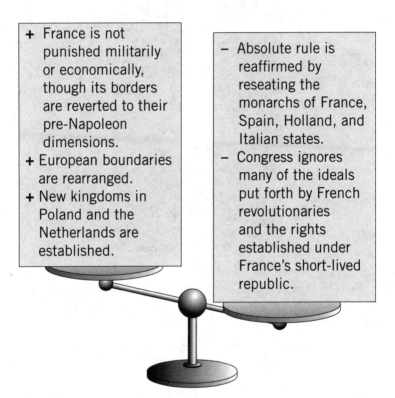

+ France is not punished militarily or economically, though its borders are reverted to their pre-Napoleon dimensions.
+ European boundaries are rearranged.
+ New kingdoms in Poland and the Netherlands are established.

– Absolute rule is reaffirmed by reseating the monarchs of France, Spain, Holland, and Italian states.
– Congress ignores many of the ideals put forth by French revolutionaries and the rights established under France's short-lived republic.

In essence, the Congress of Vienna attempted to erase the French Revolution from the collective memory of Europe and restore royal order.

The American Revolution was a colonial uprising against an imperial power, while the French Revolution involved citizens rising up against their own country's leadership. At the end of the American Revolution, Great Britain was still intact, and the new United States was in many ways modeled in the image of its former mother country. At the end of the French Revolution, however, France was a very different place. The country didn't merely lose some of its holdings; its entire sociopolitical structure changed. Even so, the American independence movement can still be described as a revolution because the United States was the first major colony to break away from European imperial power since the beginning of the Age of Exploration. What's more, the ideals of the Declaration of Independence, U.S. Constitution, and French Revolution inspired revolution all over the world.

Revolution in Latin America and Haiti

The independence movement of their neighbors to the north (the American colonists) inspired the Spanish colonies of Latin America as well as the French colony of Haiti. Although revolts had been attempted for centuries, the world order in the 19th century was ripe for revolution, and revolutionaries had greater opportunity to assert themselves.

	Mexico	Gran Colombia (modern-day Colombia, Ecuador, Venezuela)	Haiti
Before the Revolution	Spanish colony; Napoleon's invasion of Spain led to an opportunity for independence for Mexico	When Napoleon conquered Spain in 1808, he appointed his brother Joseph to the Spanish throne. Spanish colonists remained loyal to the Spanish king and did not acknowledge French rule.	French colony with thousands of slaves and plantations that served only the French crown in a mercantilist economy
During the Revolution	• **Miguel Hidalgo,** a priest, led an unsuccessful revolt in 1810. • **Jose Morelos** continued the fight but was suppressed in 1815 by the landowning class. • In 1821, landowners joined the revolution and bought into the idea of separating from Spain.	• They appointed their own leader, **Simón Bolívar,** a student of the Enlightenment. • Bolivar established a national congress and declared independence from Spain in 1811. Supporters of the crown declared civil war, leading to a decade-long struggle for freedom.	**Pierre Toussaint L'Ouverture,** a former slave, led a slave revolt that was ultimately successful due to the Haitians' fighting abilities as well as yellow fever, which claimed many French lives.

	Mexico	Gran Colombia (modern-day Colombia, Ecuador, Venezuela)	Haiti
After the Revolution	The **Treaty of Cordoba** granted independence to Mexico, marking the end of Spain's 300-year domination of Latin America.	Bolívar's vision was a huge South American country spanning the entire continent; however, the individual nation-states formed their own governments.	• **Jacques Dessalines,** also a former slave, carried on the work of L'Ouverture, who was captured and imprisoned by the French. Dessalines named himself governor-general for life and declared Haiti a free republic. • Haiti became the first Latin American nation to win its independence.

While each of these independence movements is unique, all mark a shift away from top-down governments toward a more democratic structure in which all citizens participate.

Compare Them: Revolution in the Americas and France ❗

	American 1764–1787	French 1789–1799	Haitian 1799–1804	Latin American 1810–1820s
Causes	• Unfair taxation/ war debt • Lack of representation	• Unfair taxation/ war debt • Social inequalities • Lack of representation	• French Enlightenment • Social and racial inequalities • Slave revolt	• Social inequalities • Removal of peninsulares • Napoleon's invasion of Spain
Key Events	• Boston Tea Party • Continental Congress • Declaration of Independence • Constitution and Bill of Rights	• Tennis Court Oath • National Assembly • Declaration of Rights of Man • Storming of the Bastille • Reign of Terror • Five-man Directory	• Civil war • Slave revolt • Invasion of Napoleon	• Peasant revolts • Creole revolts • Gran Colombia
Major Players	• George III • Thomas Paine • Thomas Jefferson • George Washington	• Louis XVI • Three estates • Jacobin Party • Robespierre	• Boukman • Gens de Couleur • Toussaint L'Ouverture • Napoleon Bonaparte	• Miguel Hidalgo • Simón Bolívar • José de San Martin • Emperor Pedro I
Impacts	• Independence • Federal democracy spreads— France, Haiti, Mexico	• Rise of Napoleon • Congress of Vienna • Constitutional monarchy	• Independence • Destruction of economy • Antislavery movements	• Independence • Continued inequalities • Federal democracy (Mexico) • Creole republics • Constitutional monarchy (Brazil)

Ask Yourself...

1. To what extent did the French Revolution attain its original aims?
2. Should the French, American, and Latin American revolutions be seen as part of a common worldwide trend or do the differences among them make their concurrence mere coincidence?

Industry and Imperialism 🔔

The Industrial Revolution (which began in the mid-18th century in Britain and spread rapidly through the 19th century) and Age of Imperialism (which peaked in the late 19th and early 20th centuries) are inseparable from one another. Industrial technology led to advanced weapons, which meant territories that lacked such technology could be conquered more easily. In turn, these territories became the source of raw materials with which goods and other industrial innovations were produced. Colonies also opened up new markets for goods produced by these raw materials. And on the cycle went.

As revolutionary movements became rampant in the western hemisphere, however, European powers began to look to Africa and Asia as new outlets for conquest.

The Industrial Revolution 🔔

The development of industry during this time had a huge impact on agriculture, communication, transportation, and production.

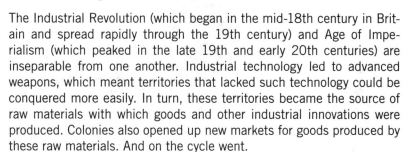

Advanced farming methods and technology cranked up farming efficiency and productivity. Through enclosure, once public lands were enclosed by fences, leading to private farming and private gain.

Increased efficiencies in farming spurred urbanization—the growth of cities. Cities usually developed in areas where resources (e.g., coal, water, and railroads) were available.

Urbanization marked a shift in the economy toward factory manufacturing, which in turn led to technological innovation.

Technological Innovations ❗

Transportation
- Steam engine (improved in 1769 by James Watt)
- Steamship (Robert Fulton, 1807)
- Steam-powered locomotive (George Stephenson, 1820s)
- Internal combustion engine (Gottlieb Daimler, 1885)

Technological Innovations

Communication
- Telegraph (Samuel Morse, 1837)
- Telephone (Alexander Graham Bell, 1876)
- Radio (Guglielmo Marconi, 1890s; based on designs of Thomas Edison, inventor of the lightbulb in 1879)

Manufacturing
- Cotton gin (Eli Whitney, 1793)
- Spinning jenny (John Hargreaves, 1764)
- Assembly line/ interchangeable parts

A Global Economy 💬

The Industrial Revolution, along with its new technologies, created the opportunity to foster transitional businesses, such as the **United Fruit Company** (an American company that sold resources from Latin American) and an Asian bank established by British bankers called the **Hong Kong and Shanghai Banking Corporation** (**HSBC**).

In order to deal with the challenges related to this new large-scale economy, several tools were put into the global marketplace:

Stock Market	Insurance	Gold Standard	Limited Liability Corporations
A system that allows private citizens to purchase and sell shares of ownership of a corporation	A service that can be purchased which allows a party to recover its losses in the event of an unexpected detrimental outcome	A monetary system allowing the world market to do business with a common currency set at a standard rate	A corporate structure that protects a company's owners from individual responsibility (liability) in the event of an unexpected detrimental outcome

---

Focus on: The Family 💬

With industrialization came significant changes to family dynamics and life. Women and children became part of the workforce, with lower wages and more dangerous working conditions than their male counterparts. Factory-run boardinghouses sprung up to house workers dependent on their employers for food, housing, and personal items. These new living conditions removed workers from their families and traditional structures.

Moreover, now that home and work were no longer centered in the same space, more delineated gender divisions emerged for the middle class. Middle-class women were expected to master the domestic sphere and remain private and separate from the realities of the working world.

New Economic and Social Philosophies

Industrialization created new socioeconomic classes.

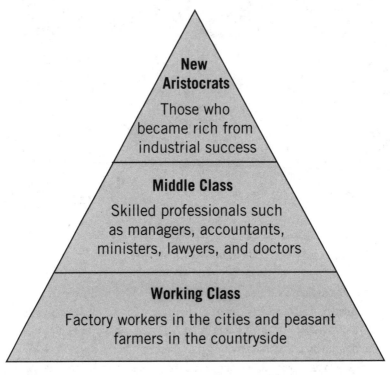

New Aristocrats
Those who became rich from industrial success

Middle Class
Skilled professionals such as managers, accountants, ministers, lawyers, and doctors

Working Class
Factory workers in the cities and peasant farmers in the countryside

Throughout history, the wealthiest people have always been the smallest portion of society, with the poorer classes making up a much greater percentage of the population. But class relations changed with industrialization. Urbanization meant people were living side by side and could see firsthand the enormous difference between the aristocracy and the working class population. What's more, members of the working class watched factory owners profit quickly, and at their expense. For the first time, people saw the connection between their sacrifices and the aristocracy's luxuries.

The questions raised by this new class structure resulted in a number of competing social and economic philosophies, specifically **laissez-faire capitalism** (a **free-market system**) and **socialism.**

Origin of Theory

Marxism (Socialism)

The foundational text of Marxism is *The Communist Manifesto* (1848), by **Karl Marx** and **Friedrich Engels.**

Capitalism (Free Market)

The foundational text of capitalism is **Adam Smith's *The Wealth of Nations*** (1776), which was a response to the mercantilist practices of European empires, in which monarchs closely managed their economies.

How Each Theory Views the Free Market

Marxism

Capitalism is inherently flawed and leads to exploitation of the working class.

Capitalism

Economic prosperity and fairness is best achieved through private ownership.

How the Economy Should Be Run

Marxism

The working class (following a revolt) controls the means of production, rendering instruments of power (the government) unnecessary.

Capitalism

Individuals, not the government, should own the means of production and sell their goods and services in an open, or free, market.

Practical Application of Theory

Marxism

This theory laid the groundwork for socialism and communism.

Capitalism

Without government control, the market would self-regulate, naturally meet societal demands, and create more opportunities for everyone.

Aside from Marxists, other political groups arose in the years following the Industrial Revolution to protect the working class and advocate reforms. **Utopian Socialists** emerged in the early 19th century, advocating use of logical appeals to industrial leaders in order to persuade them to share the means of production with the working classes. In contrast, **anarchists** rebelled against the existing institutions (both governmental and economic), advocating a working-class uprising. Pressure from both ends of the resistance spectrum ultimately led to social reforms: the British expanded suffrage, and the Germans offered pensions and public healthcare. Countries around the world established public education systems as well.

Even those who supported a free-market system could see that industrialization made way for abuses of the new working class. These people believed reforms would make capitalism more positive for all.

Capitalism + Enlightenment = Reform Catches On

Factory Act of 1883	**Labor Unions**
Limited the hours in a workday; restricted children from working in factories; required factory owners to make working conditions safer and cleaner	Formed to protect workers' rights through bargaining for better working conditions or striking to shut down production

Social Mobility

These reforms and others eventually led not only to better working conditions but also to improved standards of living on the individual family level. As a result, the middle class increased in size, and **social mobility**—the ability to work one's way up to a higher socioeconomic class—became more commonplace.

Increased social mobility is in some ways connected to the emergence of **Social Darwinism**. This philosophy applied Charles Darwin's biological theory of natural selection to society, claiming that those who were naturally superior would rise to the top through the process of "survival of the fittest." Social Darwinism was also used to explain the dominance of white people.

Rudyard Kipling took this a step further in his poem "**The White Man's Burden**." According to Kipling, Europeans, as naturally superior beings, were morally obligated to conquer native peoples and "civilize" them. And so the foundation was laid for European imperialism.

European Ethnocentrism

Ethnocentrism—the belief in the inherent superiority of one's ethnic group or culture—is not unique to imperialist Europe, but its ethnocentric attitudes did take on a new danger due to its ability and willingness to act on those attitudes. Armed with the most technologically advanced militaries and strong economic motives, the Europeans were quite capable of subjugating people whom they considered to be inferior, barbaric, or dispensable. Their success at doing so reinforced ethnocentric attitudes, leading to further colonialism and subjugation.

European Imperialism in India ❗

This 1888 cartoon depicts John Bull (the personification of Great Britain—think of him as the British Uncle Sam). Here, the British Empire has its "hands" all over the world, from Australia to North America (Canada and Jamaica) to Africa (Boersland and Egypt).

While the Industrial Revolution certainly brought wealth to the West, it also hit Asia's less advanced industries hard, such as shipbuilding (India, Southeast Asia) and iron-working (India). On the other hand, many parts of Asia still thrived economically due to global demand: opium production remained strong in south and central Asia, and India continued to "clothe the world" with its cotton fields.

As Europe industrialized, it looked to its colonies to supply the raw materials and act as a secondary market for its products. This advantageous relationship is demonstrated in the case of India as a British colony.

The Beginnings of Imperialism in India ❗

- During the Seven Years' War, the **British East India Company,** led by Robert Clive, raised an army that drove the French out of India.
- Over the next 100 years, various administrative regions were set up throughout the empire, which were controlled by company-sponsored troops.
- The East India Company relied on **Sepoys,** Indians who worked for the British, mainly as soldiers.

The Sepoy Mutiny ❗

Cause	The Mutiny	Effect
By the mid-1800s, the Sepoys had become alarmed by the British's territorial greed, as well as their lack of respect for Indian culture and religious customs.*	Fighting went on for nearly two years, but the rebellion ultimately failed.	British parliament stepped in, took control of India away from the East India Company, making all of India a crown colony directly run by the British government.

In 1857, the Sepoys learned that their bullet cartridges—which had to be bitten off in order to load into rifles—were greased with pork and beef fat. This was a direct violation of Muslim and Hindu dietary laws. This was the last straw, and the Sepoys rebelled.

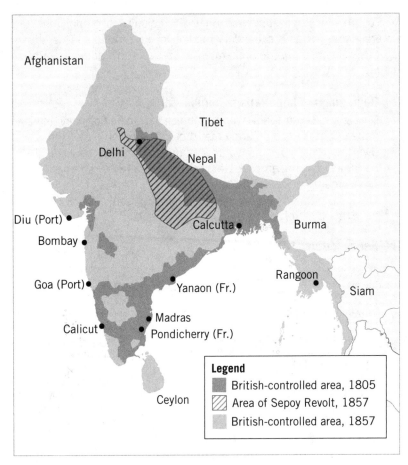

British Rule in India c. 1857

Full-Blown Colonialism ⚠

India became the model of British imperialism at the expense of Indian culture and institutions. A mercantilist economy was established, urbanization took hold, Christianity spread, and the upper castes were taught English.

Anglicization of the upper castes has consequences, however: access to education allowed them to become more sophisticated in their world view and dream of freeing India from British rule.

Indian National Congress formed in 1885 by a group of highly educated Indians to start a path toward independence; they are unsuccessful until after World War II.

 Ask Yourself...

1. How did Europe use ethnocentrism to achieve their colonialist aims?
2. Was the colonization of India a relatively peaceful expansion? Were there any benefits for India to being a British colony?

European Imperialism in China 🛑

For much of its history, China was relatively isolationist and placed strict limitations on what could be traded. This all changed during the Age of Imperialism as the European powers gained industrial muscle and worked their way in. China's instability didn't help matters. By the end of the 19th century, Britain, France, Germany, and Russia had established **spheres of influence** in China, carving the country up for themselves.

1773	Early to Mid-1800s	1838

British traders introduce opium to China.

Internal rebellion erupts in an unstable China. Buddhists upset over taxes and government corruption lead the **White Lotus Rebellions** at the beginning of the century. In the middle of the century, the **Taiping Rebellion** nearly succeeds in bringing down the Manchu government.

Opium is banned due to widespread addiction to the drug among the Chinese, upsetting the British.

1899–1901	1899

In the **Boxer Rebellion,** a pro-nationalist and anti-European militia (later known as Boxers) rise up in response to the Manchu government's defeats and concessions to Europe. Using guerrilla tactics, they kill Christian missionaries and seize foreign embassies. The uprising fails, however, and China is forced to sign the **Boxer Protocol,** which demands the Chinese pay for the costs of the rebellion and formally apologize for it.

Worried that they would lose their influence in China to the European powers, the United States implements the **Open Door Policy,** in which they pledged their support of China's sovereignty and announce equal trading privileges among all imperial powers (i.e., Europe and the United States).

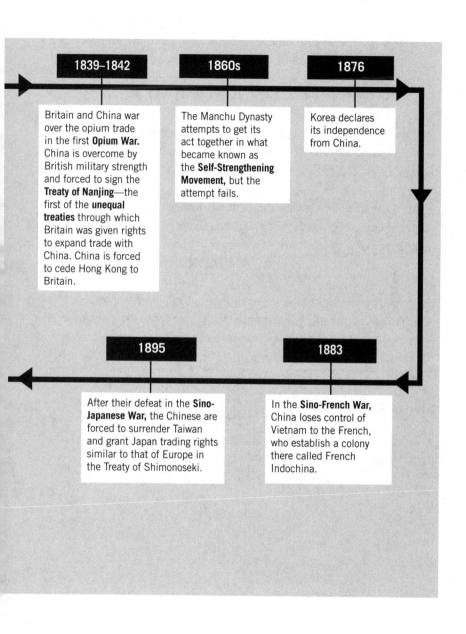

1839–1842

Britain and China war over the opium trade in the first **Opium War.** China is overcome by British military strength and forced to sign the **Treaty of Nanjing**—the first of the **unequal treaties** through which Britain was given rights to expand trade with China. China is forced to cede Hong Kong to Britain.

1860s

The Manchu Dynasty attempts to get its act together in what became known as the **Self-Strengthening Movement,** but the attempt fails.

1876

Korea declares its independence from China.

1895

After their defeat in the **Sino-Japanese War,** the Chinese are forced to surrender Taiwan and grant Japan trading rights similar to that of Europe in the Treaty of Shimonoseki.

1883

In the **Sino-French War,** China loses control of Vietnam to the French, who establish a colony there called French Indochina.

By 1911, the Chinese government would topple. But more on that later.

Contrast Them: Imperialism in China and in India

Multiple countries originally traded with India, but the British won out and established exclusive control. In China, Britain dominated trade early on, and as they succeeded, more and more countries piled on.

In India, the British established a true colony, running the government and directing huge internal projects. In China, the European powers and Japan established spheres of influence, focusing on the economic benefits of trade with no overall governmental responsibilities.

Therefore, when independence movements began in India, the efforts were directed against Britain, the foreign occupier. In contrast, when the Chinese people wanted change, they targeted their own government—the Manchu Dynasty.

Japanese Imperialism

Japan remained isolationist during the 17th and 18th centuries and successfully kept out European influences. By the 19th century, however, it was difficult to keep westerners at bay due to their industrial power and desire for markets.

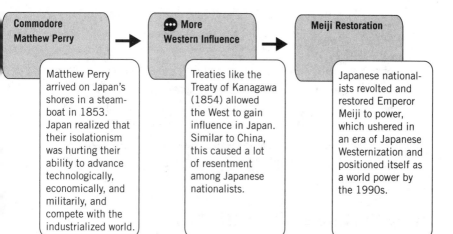

Commodore Matthew Perry

Matthew Perry arrived on Japan's shores in a steamboat in 1853. Japan realized that their isolationism was hurting their ability to advance technologically, economically, and militarily, and compete with the industrialized world.

💬 More Western Influence

Treaties like the Treaty of Kanagawa (1854) allowed the West to gain influence in Japan. Similar to China, this caused a lot of resentment among Japanese nationalists.

Meiji Restoration

Japanese nationalists revolted and restored Emperor Meiji to power, which ushered in an era of Japanese Westernization and positioned itself as a world power by the 1990s.

Contrast Them: The Industrial Revolution in Europe and Japan

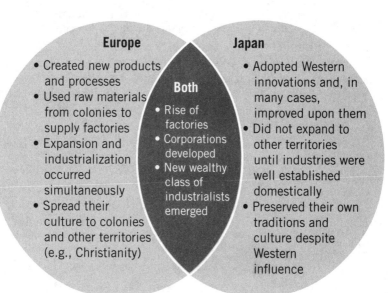

Europe
- Created new products and processes
- Used raw materials from colonies to supply factories
- Expansion and industrialization occurred simultaneously
- Spread their culture to colonies and other territories (e.g., Christianity)

Both
- Rise of factories
- Corporations developed
- New wealthy class of industrialists emerged

Japan
- Adopted Western innovations and, in many cases, improved upon them
- Did not expand to other territories until industries were well established domestically
- Preserved their own traditions and culture despite Western influence

The industrialization of Europe and Japan followed very similar paths, but Japan's was on fast forward. The country managed to accomplish in only a few decades what had taken Europe more than a century, in large part because it didn't have to invent everything itself—it just needed to implement the advances of Western industrialization. Still, the pattern was remarkably similar: private corporations rose up, industrialists like the Mitsubishi family became wealthy, factories were built, urbanization increased dramatically, and reforms were implemented. Japan learned from Europe quite well. After all, if you can't beat them, join them.

European Imperialism in Africa

End of the Slave Trade

During the Age of Exploration, Europe turned an eye to Africa. Its coastal regions were important strategically for trade, and the continent as a whole became the center of the slave trade. As Enlightenment principles took hold in Europe, however, more and more people opposed slavery. Most European nations abolished the slave trade between 1807 and 1820, though the practice itself continued until the mid-19th century. But even with no slave trade, the European powers will still hungry for Africa's natural resources.

South Africa

The **Boer War** (1899–1902) was a series of battles between the British and South African Dutch (Boers) after diamonds and gold* were discovered in the Transvaal region. The British won, and South Africa became part of the British Empire.

Africans were not allowed access to these resources, of course, and forced to work in the mines while the diamonds and gold were sold abroad.

Egypt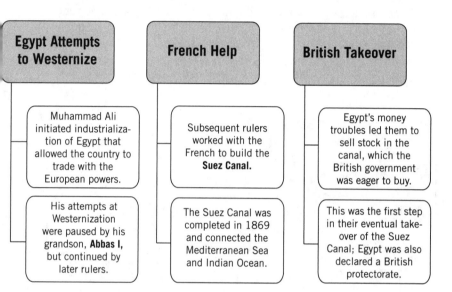

The Ottomans ruled Egypt for centuries, though their rule was extremely weak throughout the 19th century. Napoleon tried to conquer Egypt during this time but was fought off by **Muhammad Ali,** who also defeated the Ottomans and subsequently gained control of Egypt in 1805.

Egypt Attempts to Westernize	French Help	British Takeover
Muhammad Ali initiated industrialization of Egypt that allowed the country to trade with the European powers.	Subsequent rulers worked with the French to build the **Suez Canal.**	Egypt's money troubles led them to sell stock in the canal, which the British government was eager to buy.
His attempts at Westernization were paused by his grandson, **Abbas I,** but continued by later rulers.	The Suez Canal was completed in 1869 and connected the Mediterranean Sea and Indian Ocean.	This was the first step in their eventual takeover of the Suez Canal; Egypt was also declared a British protectorate.

Pushed out, the French looked to other parts of North Africa, which was also of interest to Italy.

The Berlin Conference: Carving Up the Continent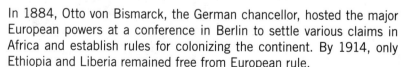

In 1884, Otto von Bismarck, the German chancellor, hosted the major European powers at a conference in Berlin to settle various claims in Africa and establish rules for colonizing the continent. By 1914, only Ethiopia and Liberia remained free from European rule.

Although colonization added infrastructure and self-rule was permitted (in the case of the British colonies), the consequences for the continent were enormous.

- Africa was stripped of its resources.
- Natives were treated harshly.
- Traditional tribal boundary lines were disrupted. In some situations, tribal lands were divided among different European powers; in other cases, rival tribes were unwillingly brought together under the same colonial ruler.
- African culture and traditions were eroded with the influence of Christian missionaries, European schools, and western business practices.

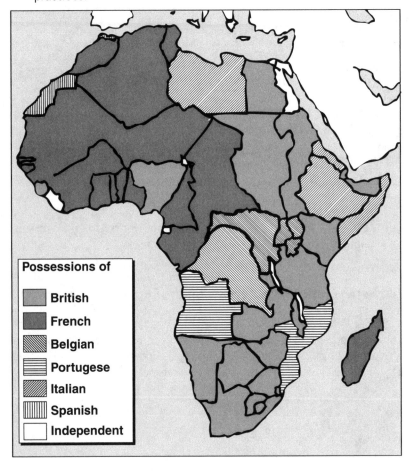

European Colonies in Africa, 1914

European Colonialism in Africa vs. Latin America

Colonialism in Africa was similar to that in the Americas in that boundary lines were determined by European agreements from abroad: there was a total disregard for the societies that existed in the regions before. Moreover, in both places, multiple countries held claims to the land. With the exception of the British-controlled colonies, African colonies were governed by direct rule, similar to European rule of colonies in the Americas. This meant that European officials were sent to occupy all positions of authority. Native traditions were disregarded. This contrasts with the spheres of influence in China, for example; in that case, Europeans were generally more interested in making money than changing the culture.

Resistance to Colonialism

Colonized peoples did not typically welcome the imperialist powers with open arms. Resistance came in different forms. In some cases, resistance to imperialism was violent.

Resistance Against Mughal India	Resistance Against the Manchus
Resisting group: Marathas (Hindus from the state of Maharashtra)	Resisting group: Taiping Heavenly Kingdom
Resistance: A 27-year war (1680–1708) greatly decreased Mughal power, paving the way for the Maratha Empire.	Resistance: During the Qing Dynasty, the Taiping Heavenly Kingdom waged a 14-year war (1850–1864) against the Manchus. While the Qing Dynasty emerged victorious, the struggle greatly diminished its power.

In other cases, imperialism inspired colonized peoples to develop nationalist movements:

Nation	Location	Rebelled against
Cherokee	Southern United States	United States government
Zulu	South Africa	British government
Balkan states	Southeastern Europe	Ottoman Empire and Austro-Hungarian Empire

 Ask Yourself...

1. In what ways did the impact of European colonialism differ in Asia and in Africa?
2. Why was Japan unique in Asia in terms of its ability to become a colonial power rather that a colonized nation?

Nationalist Movements and Other Developments ❗

Another effect of industrialization on the European continent was a shift in the balance of power among countries. Industrialization strengthened European powers and empires that were already dominant (France, Spain, Portugal, Britain, and Russia), while also allowing smaller European nations to gain independence and "a seat at the table." The unification of the Italian and German city-states is a prime example of this.

Challenges to Unification	• Relied on foreign military forces to overthrow existing government • Borders were never solidly defined • Difficult to unify regional cultural differences
Benefits of Unification	• Italy able to assert its regional independence, which becomes important during World Wars I and II • Helped to limit the expansion of colonialism within Europe

Unification of Italy ❗

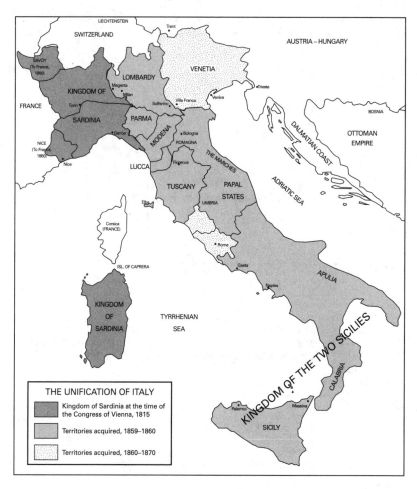

The Unification of Italy

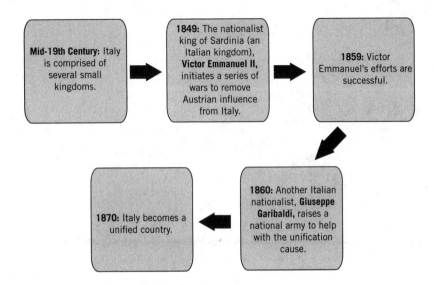

Mid-19th Century: Italy is comprised of several small kingdoms.

1849: The nationalist king of Sardinia (an Italian kingdom), **Victor Emmanuel II,** initiates a series of wars to remove Austrian influence from Italy.

1859: Victor Emmanuel's efforts are successful.

1870: Italy becomes a unified country.

1860: Another Italian nationalist, **Giuseppe Garibaldi,** raises a national army to help with the unification cause.

Unification of Germany

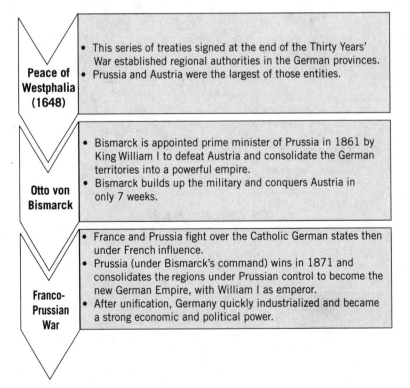

Peace of Westphalia (1648)
- This series of treaties signed at the end of the Thirty Years' War established regional authorities in the German provinces.
- Prussia and Austria were the largest of those entities.

Otto von Bismarck
- Bismarck is appointed prime minister of Prussia in 1861 by King William I to defeat Austria and consolidate the German territories into a powerful empire.
- Bismarck builds up the military and conquers Austria in only 7 weeks.

Franco-Prussian War
- France and Prussia fight over the Catholic German states then under French influence.
- Prussia (under Bismarck's command) wins in 1871 and consolidates the regions under Prussian control to become the new German Empire, with William I as emperor.
- After unification, Germany quickly industrialized and became a strong economic and political power.

Other Political Developments

Russia	Ottoman Empire	United States
• **Emancipation Edict:** Issued by czar **Alexander II,** the edict essentially abolished serfdom but did little good. Serfs were given small plots of land that they had to pay the government to keep, so it was difficult for them to improve their lot. Some serfs moved to cities to work in Russia's rising industries but faced harsh working conditions. • **Russification:** This nationalist policy was implemented by Czar Alexander III, following the assassination of Alexander II by a political group (The People's Will) that opposed the monarchy. All Russians, including those in far-flung areas who did not share a Russian cultural history, were expected to learn the language and convert to Russian Orthodoxy. Anyone who did not comply was persecuted.	• **Looming Decline** *17th–18th century:* Ottomans continually fought the Russians for control of the Balkans, Black Sea, and surrounding areas. Russians are victorious most of the time. *19th century:* Britain and France tried to keep the weakened Ottoman Empire going in order to stop Russian expansion (i.e., Crimean War of 1853) while also increasing their own influence in the region (e.g., Britain gained control of Egypt in 1882).	• **Monroe Doctrine (1823)*:** In an effort to prevent European interference and colonization in the Americas, President Monroe declares the Western Hemisphere off limits to Europe. • **Panama Canal:** The United States incited people in Panama to declare their independence from Colombia so that the U.S. government could negotiate the right to build the Panama Canal. Many Latin Americans saw this as the United States exercising its own form of imperialism—the Monroe Doctrine gone too far. • **Spanish-American War (1898):** Spain lost its foothold in the Western Hemisphere, as the United States helped Cuba gain its independence from Spain and gained control of Guam, the Philippines, and Puerto Rico. The outcome of the war helps establish the United States as a world power.

In 1904, President Theodore Roosevelt issued what came to be known as the **Roosevelt Corollary to the Monroe Doctrine,** which provided that the United States would intervene in financial disputes between European powers and Latin American nations if doing so were essential to maintaining peace.

Ask Yourself...

What measures did different nations take to solidify a sense of national identity among its people?

Early Feminism

The opportunity to demand the full rights of citizenship during this period of reform was not lost on suffragettes, philosophers, and other advocates for women's rights. Three key 19th-century documents that jump-started the feminist movements of the 20th century are:

Declaration of the Rights of Woman and the Female Citizen	A Vindication of the Rights of Woman	Declaration of Sentiments
• 1791 • Written by Olympe de Gouges (France) • A response to the French National Assembly's "Declaration of the Rights of Man and the Citizen" in the lead up to the French Revolution • The pamphlet led to Gouges being convicted of treason and ultimlatey executed during the Reign of Terror.	• 1792 • Written by Mary Wollstonecraft (England) • Advocates for educational opportunities for women, asserting the importance of women in society as child educators themselves • "Humanized" women by asserting that women should be seen as citizens with equal rights rather than possessions of their husbands and fathers.	• 1848 • Written by Elizabeth Cady Stanton (United States), among others • Very closely paralleling the United States Declaration of Independence, the document lists grievances held by women who had long endured unequal treatement. • It was signed by both women and men who attended the Seneca Falls Convention, the first women's rights assembly to be organized by women.

Ask Yourself...

How has the definition and perception of feminism evolved since the 19th century? Can you think of some big moments for feminism over the last several decades?

Period 5: Key Takeaways and Themes 💥

Industrialization essentially changed the global landscape and fueled imperialism, which fueled further industrialization in return.

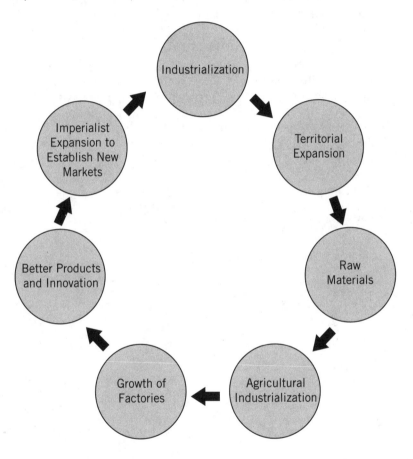

Pros of Industrialization	Cons of Industrialization
• Increase in unskilled labor creates job opportunities. • More efficient production (thanks to the assembly line, in part) and transportation meets demands of the expanding global market and improves standard of living for some. • Arts and culture flourish (Impressionist movement, cubism, surrealism, art nouveau). • Middle- and upper-class housewives were able to dedicate more time to intellectual and political pursuits, setting the stage for the women's suffrage movement of the early 20th century. Some working-class women, meanwhile, became involved in workers' rights and labor unions.	• Factory workers faced harsh working conditions and low wages. • Further stratification occurred between the rich and the poor. • Industrialization drove imperialism and exploitation of resources in the colonies. • It led to the development of more destructive weapons, which allowed for massive devastation on the World War battlefields. • The majority of women were still denied access to education due to ideas of mental inferiority based on social Darwinism.

Ask Yourself...

What are some other pros of industrialization? Other cons? Write them in the space provided in the table.

From 1750 to 1900, so much happened in so many different places that it's easy to get lost. You can use the following flowchart to help connect the dots between events, or use it as a starting point to create your own!

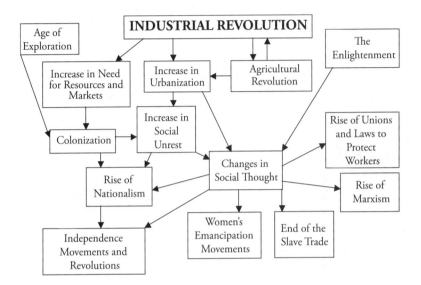

Another theme of this time period is the growing tendency toward nationalism and independence, from the revolutions in America and France to the unification of the Italian kingdoms and German territories. People all over the world began to identify strongly with their nation or dream of the creation of their own nation.

Finally, it's important to keep in mind the often conflicting motives of the individuals and governments effecting change during this period. The United States, for example, declared its independence from Britain only to wield a heavy hand in Latin American affairs by the end of the 19th century. Change is indeed very complex, and during this time period, life changed for nearly everyone on the globe. By 1900, the world was a very different place.

 Ask Yourself...

Do you think that the revolutions, calls for equality, and developments of nationalism mentioned in this chapter would have inevitably occurred even without the Industrial Revolution? Why or why not?

PERIOD 6

c. 1900 to Present

The 20th century saw rapid changes in global power. Two world wars transferred world power from Europe to the United States and put an end to the era of colonialism. Globalization in the post-colonial world is a story that continues to be written today, but its impact in Asia, Africa, and Latin America has already shaped some of the major events of the 21st century.

The 20th Century: Accelerating Global Change and Realignments

At the beginning of the 20th century, most of the world was either colonized by Europe or had once been colonized by Europe. This meant that everyone in the world was connected to the instability of that small but powerful continent. It also meant that when European powers were at war with each other, their colonies were dragged into the fight.

The World War I Era

In 1914, a major conflict among European powers had a substantial and destructive effect on the rest of the world.

Start of World War I

Many teachers sort out the causes of World War I by using the acronym MAIN:

Militarism
Alliance system
Industrialism
Nationalism

These four factors created a powder keg in Europe, and it needed only a single match to be thrown into it to create a chaotic era—the likes of which the continent had never seen.

Alliance System

In the decades leading up to World War I, the European powers tried to keep the balance of power in check by forming alliances. The newly unified Germany quickly gained industrial might, but it was worried that France, its archenemy since the Franco-Prussian War in 1870, would seek revenge for its defeat. Before he resigned from office, Otto von Bismarck created and negotiated the **Triple Alliance**.

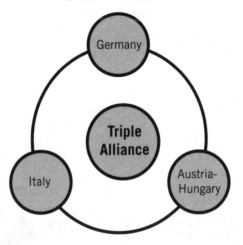

In response, France allied with Russia, a situation that sandwiched Germany between two opponents. The two countries also signed friendly agreements with Great Britain to become the **Triple Entente**.

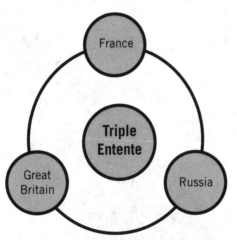

The alliance system was created in such a way that countries with no acrimonious issues between them could conceivably be pulled into war because they had a pact to defend a country that had a pact to defend yet another country that had gone to war with a country that also had pacts with other nations. (Whew!)

In 1914, **Archduke Franz Ferdinand** of Austria-Hungary visited Sarajevo, the capital of Bosnia. Sarajevo consisted of Serbs who wished for inclusion in the nation of Serbia. **Gavrilo Princip**, a Serbian nationalist, shot and killed the Archduke and his wife. This caused a geopolitical domino effect*:

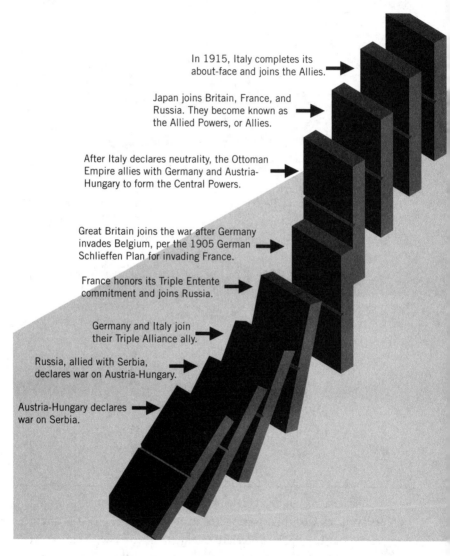

In 1915, Italy completes its about-face and joins the Allies.

Japan joins Britain, France, and Russia. They become known as the Allied Powers, or Allies.

After Italy declares neutrality, the Ottoman Empire allies with Germany and Austria-Hungary to form the Central Powers.

Great Britain joins the war after Germany invades Belgium, per the 1905 German Schlieffen Plan for invading France.

France honors its Triple Entente commitment and joins Russia.

Germany and Italy join their Triple Alliance ally.

Russia, allied with Serbia, declares war on Austria-Hungary.

Austria-Hungary declares war on Serbia.

 Pro tip: Read this diagram from the bottom left to the top right!

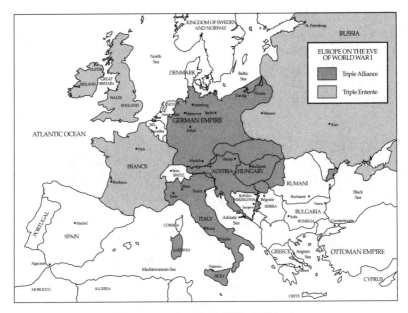

Europe on the Eve of World War I

Isolationism to War 🛑

As World War I began to brew, the United States made an effort to stay out of the conflict. Focusing on its own interests and pursuing a policy of **isolationism**, the United States declared neutrality. However, public pressure mounted following the German submarine attack on the British passenger ship *Lusitania*, which carried over 100 Americans. Tensions escalated further when German submarines (known as U-boats) attacked U.S. merchant ships en route to Great Britain.

The following cartoon depicts the **Zimmerman telegram,** a secret message sent between German officials that suggested Mexico might have wanted to join forces with Germany to regain the territory it had lost to the United States in 1846. The Germans reasoned that a war with Mexico would keep the United States out of the European war. Americans were outraged and the country declared war on Germany in 1917.

"The Temptation." Published March 2, 1917

A New Kind of War

The Industrial Revolution had given Europe some powerful new weapons, plus the ships and airplanes that were often needed to deliver them. Moreover, large industrial cities had millions of people, creating the possibility of massive casualties in a single bombing raid. 20th-century technology combined with a 19th-century approach to war led to 8.5 million deaths. World War I introduced new war technology and techniques, including tanks, airplanes, trench warfare, and firebombing.

End of the War 🔔

On November 11, 1918, after brutal battles, trench warfare, and enormous loss of life, Germany and the Central Powers finally gave up. Signed in 1919, the **Treaty of Versailles** brought an official end to World War I. American President Woodrow Wilson proposed the **Fourteen Points** plan, but it was largely modified by Britain and France, which needed to justify the human and financial cost of the war and the duration of the war to their demoralized populations. The resulting treaty was extremely punitive against Germany, which was humiliated by having to admit full responsibility for the war.

Fourteen Points		
Issue	What Wilson Suggested	What Ended Up in the Treaty
Economy	Free trade and lower tariffs	Germany must pay war costs.
Militarism	Reduction of arms	Germany forced to disarm; the Allies did not have to disarm.
Imperialism	End of colonialism	The German colonies were split up among the Allies.
Diplomacy	**League of Nations** to promote peaceful, diplomatic resolutions to international conflicts	• The League of Nations was created, but it lacked authority (no armed force), was inefficient (action required unanimous votes), and lacked moral credibility (criticized as a "League of Victors"). • The United States Senate did not allow an American presence in the League of Nations, much to President Wilson's disappointment.

Russian Revolution ❗

During the First World War, the Russians enacted a revolution that so disrupted the country it had to exit the war early.

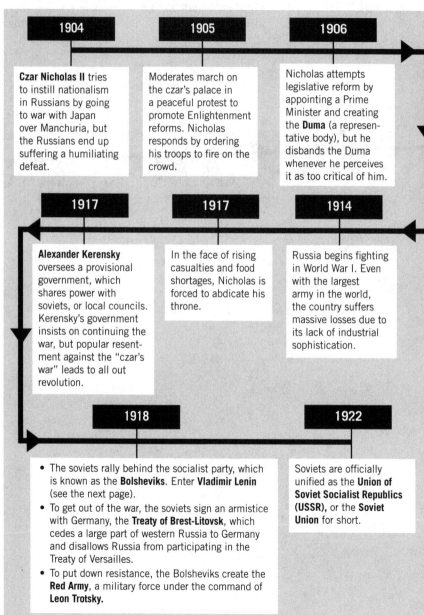

1904

Czar Nicholas II tries to instill nationalism in Russians by going to war with Japan over Manchuria, but the Russians end up suffering a humiliating defeat.

1905

Moderates march on the czar's palace in a peaceful protest to promote Enlightenment reforms. Nicholas responds by ordering his troops to fire on the crowd.

1906

Nicholas attempts legislative reform by appointing a Prime Minister and creating the **Duma** (a representative body), but he disbands the Duma whenever he perceives it as too critical of him.

1917

Alexander Kerensky oversees a provisional government, which shares power with soviets, or local councils. Kerensky's government insists on continuing the war, but popular resentment against the "czar's war" leads to all out revolution.

1917

In the face of rising casualties and food shortages, Nicholas is forced to abdicate his throne.

1914

Russia begins fighting in World War I. Even with the largest army in the world, the country suffers massive losses due to its lack of industrial sophistication.

1918

- The soviets rally behind the socialist party, which is known as the **Bolsheviks**. Enter **Vladimir Lenin** (see the next page).
- To get out of the war, the soviets sign an armistice with Germany, the **Treaty of Brest-Litovsk**, which cedes a large part of western Russia to Germany and disallows Russia from participating in the Treaty of Versailles.
- To put down resistance, the Bolsheviks create the **Red Army**, a military force under the command of **Leon Trotsky.**

1922

Soviets are officially unified as the **Union of Soviet Socialist Republics (USSR),** or the **Soviet Union** for short.

- Marxist leader of the Bolsheviks who mobilized the support of workers and soldiers
- Issued the **April Theses,** which demanded peace, land for peasants, and power to the soviets
- Under his vision of mass socialization, set about nationalizing the assets and industries of Russia
- Instituted the **New Economic Policy (NEP)** in the early 1920s, which had some capitalistic aspects, such as allowing farmers to sell portions of their grain for their own profit

Creation of Turkey ❶

The Ottoman Empire, known at the time as the "Sick Man of Europe," made a fatal mistake by joining the Central Powers. The Ottomans ceded most of their remaining land following the war and were thus vulnerable for attack from the newly armed Greeks. The Turks were not going to take the mistakes of the Ottoman Empire lying down, and **Mustafa Kemal** assured that it wouldn't.

- Known as **Ataturk,** "the Father of the Turks"
- Led successful military attacks against the Greeks and overthrew the Ottoman sultan
- Became the first president of modern Turkey in 1923
- Instituted reforms to modernize Turkey (at times with ruthless brutality)
  - Secularized the Muslim nation
  - Introduced Western-style dress and legal code (as opposed to an Islamic one)
  - Changed alphabet from Arabic to Latin
  - Established a parliamentary system

The World War II Era 🔴

Although World War II did not begin until 1939, its causes were already well underway in the 1920s. As such, World War II isn't so much a distinct war from World War I but rather the Great War Part II.

Soviet Union 🔴

Lenin's New Economic Plan (NEP) was successful for agriculture, but Lenin died before he could incorporate the NEP into other parts of the Soviet economy. Following Lenin's death, the Communist Party turned to **Joseph Stalin**.

Joseph Stalin and Collectivization 🔴

Joseph Stalin resented the slow pace of the NEP and resolved to speed up the development of a communist nation through **collectivization**: aggressively overtaking private farms and turning them into state-owned enterprises.

Five-Year Plans 🔴

Collectivization was achieved through Stalin's **Five-Year Plans**. From 1928 until 1932, Stalin used Five-Year Plans to attempt to create his ambition of **Socialism in One Country**, a blueprint for developing the industrial and military might of the USSR*, before spreading the system to other countries abroad.

Just a heads up: Soviet Union and USSR are used interchangeably throughout this chapter.

ASAP World History

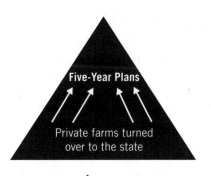

Five-Year Plans

Private farms turned over to the state

Five-Year Plans *seemed* communist because
- the state owned the means of production
- the state owned farms
- large, nationalized factories were constructed

Five-Year Plans were *actually* totalitarian because
- the people didn't share in the power or the profits
- the people had no choice regarding participation

The Violence of Five-Year Plans*

- Untold numbers died fighting to protect their farms.
- Even more people died in famines caused by Stalin usurping crops to feed government workers at the expense of the farmers themselves.

 Not to be confused with the kind of five-year plan that involves graduating high school, attending college, getting a job, and maybe buying a car.

United States 📢

In the years following World War I, the United States was in a position to fund much of Europe's recovery. The financial headquarters of the world shifted from London to New York City, which had become a major center of credit to Europe. In other words, the United States loaned money to Europe, and lots of it.

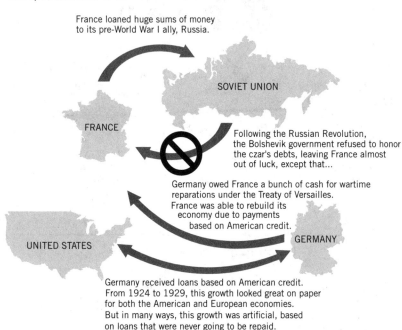

France loaned huge sums of money to its pre-World War I ally, Russia.

SOVIET UNION

FRANCE

Following the Russian Revolution, the Bolshevik government refused to honor the czar's debts, leaving France almost out of luck, except that...

Germany owed France a bunch of cash for wartime reparations under the Treaty of Versailles. France was able to rebuild its economy due to payments based on American credit.

UNITED STATES

GERMANY

Germany received loans based on American credit. From 1924 to 1929, this growth looked great on paper for both the American and European economies. But in many ways, this growth was artificial, based on loans that were never going to be repaid.

The Great Depression 📢

When the U.S. stock market crashed in October 1929, a spiral of monetary and fiscal problems called the **Great Depression** quickly escalated into an international catastrophe.

- American banks stopped extending credit.
- Germany couldn't pay back war reparations, so France also had no money.
- Europe ran out of money (which it never really had in the first place).

Franklin Roosevelt 🔱

The United States and Germany were hit hardest by the Great Depression. In both countries, almost one-third of the work force was unemployed. In the United States, out-of-work Americans rejected the dominant party and in 1932, elected **Franklin Roosevelt** as president in a landslide election.

Italy and the Rise of Fascism 🔱

Countries without long-standing democratic traditions, such as Germany and Italy, went in a direction that allowed for the triumph of an ideology anathema to the spirit of democracy. Between World Wars I and II, fascist parties emerged across Europe. The main idea of **fascism** was to destroy the will of the individual in favor of "the people." Fascists pushed for an identity rooted in extreme nationalism, which often relied on racial identity.

Italy was the first state to have a fascist government. The founder and leader was **Benito Mussolini.**

Key People: Benito Mussolini

- 1919—Mussolini creates the National Fascist Party.
- 1921—The Party wins its first seats in the Italian parliament.
- 1922
    - Mussolini marches on Rome with party members to demand cabinet appointments from King Victor Emmanuel III. The king, who could easily put an end to the demands, refuses to declare martial law.
    - Mussolini is appointed prime minister by the king. He eventually takes total control of the government after a short stint as parliamentary leader.
- 1923—He orders the invasion of the Greek island of Corfu, calling the League of Nations' bluff as a feckless organization.

- 1926—Following a number of assassination attempts, Mussolini declares all other parties illegal, transforming Italy into a totalitarian fascist regime.
- 1935—Italy invades Ethiopia, part of a pattern of expansion in Africa as a means to rally the Italian people behind a nationalist cause.

The Fascist party paid squads known as **Blackshirts** to fight socialist and communist organizations, an action that won over the loyalty of both factory owners and landowners.

Germany 🛈

Following Germany's defeat in World War I, there was a power vacuum in the German government. Workers' and soldiers' councils (not unlike Russian soviets) formed in cities like Berlin. Some workers' councils advocated communist or socialist systems. However, because Germany's middle class was quite conservative and many Germans had been relatively prosperous before the war, socialism was rejected in favor of a fairly conservative democratic republic called the **Weimar Republic**.

Nazis 🛈

Despite the stability of a democratic republic, anti-democratic forces expanded their influence in the 1920s—namely, the **National Socialist Party (Nazis)**.

What Made Nazism Possible?

CAUSES:
- Germany was in economic crisis.

- Mussolini's influence was expanding into Germany.

- Germans resented the harsh reparations placed on them by the Treaty of Versailles, which had further weakened the German economy.

RESULT:
German people increasingly rejected the solutions of the Weimar Republic's elected body, the **Reichstag.**

Key People: Adolf Hitler

- Hitler rose to power as head of the Nazi Party in 1921.
- In 1924, he attempted to enact his own "March on Rome" (a la Mussolini) and led Nazis in a raid of a public meeting, known as the Beer Hall Putsch. Hitler was imprisoned for a year, during which time he penned his manifesto, *Mein Kampf,* outlining his political views and anti-Semitism.
- Like Mussolini's fascism, Hitler's Nazism inspired extreme nationalism and dreams of renewed greatness for a depressed and divided country.
- Hitler emphasized the superiority of one race (Aryans) over others, particularly Slavs and Jews, who had "corrupted" the German race.
- He argued that Jews should be deported (later changed to "eliminated") and that Germans should take over Europe.

Third Reich ❗

Even though the Nazis initially operated as any other party in the Reichstag (gaining votes democratically), their popularity soon enabled Germany's slide into a totalitarian state. Hitler's rise to power coincided with the declining German economy:

As the Great Depression further sank Germany's economy in 1930, the Nazis increased their seats in the Reichstag tenfold that year.	In 1933, Hitler was elected chancellor (leader of the Reichstag) and soon seized control of the government.	Hitler's fascist rule was known as the **Third Reich**—a reference to previous German regimes set on conquering Europe.	In violation of the Treaty of Versailles, Hitler began to rebuild the Germany military and withdrew from the League of Nations.

German Expansion 💬

Hitler embarked on a mission to restore Germany to its former world-power status through a series of military actions. In 1935, Hitler recaptured the **Rhineland**, a region of Germany lost in World War I. Then, in 1938, Hitler annexed Austria and moved to invade a region of Czechoslovakia known as the **Sudetenland.**

Munich Conference 💬

In 1938, Hitler, Mussolini, and British Prime Minister **Neville Chamberlain** met in Munich to discuss Germany's recent invasions.

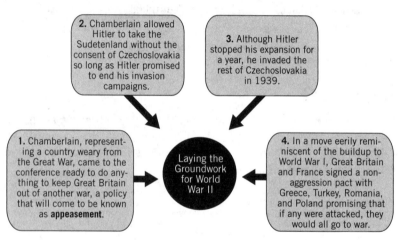

2. Chamberlain allowed Hitler to take the Sudetenland without the consent of Czechoslovakia so long as Hitler promised to end his invasion campaigns.

3. Although Hitler stopped his expansion for a year, he invaded the rest of Czechoslovakia in 1939.

1. Chamberlain, representing a country weary from the Great War, came to the conference ready to do anything to keep Great Britain out of another war, a policy that will come to be known as **appeasement.**

Laying the Groundwork for World War II

4. In a move eerily reminiscent of the buildup to World War I, Great Britain and France signed a non-aggression pact with Greece, Turkey, Romania, and Poland promising that if any were attacked, they would all go to war.

Nazi-Soviet Pact 💬

In August 1939, Hitler and Stalin signed an agreement, the **Nazi-Soviet Pact,** that would lead the world into its second Great War of the century. The main points of this agreement were as follows:

- Germany would not invade the Soviet Union as long as the Soviet Union did not interfere in Germany's expansion efforts.
- Eastern Europe would be divided between Germany and the Soviet Union.

With this secure agreement with the Soviet Union, Germany marched into Poland unencumbered. Two days later, Britain realized that all diplomacy had failed and declared war on Germany, with France reluctantly following suit.

Meanwhile, in Japan... ❗

Following the Meiji Restoration, Japan defeated China in a war for control of Korea and Taiwan and then spent several decades becoming not just an imperial power, but a world power.

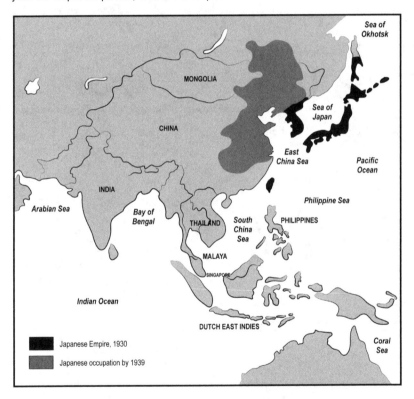

Japanese Territory by 1939

How Japan Got There

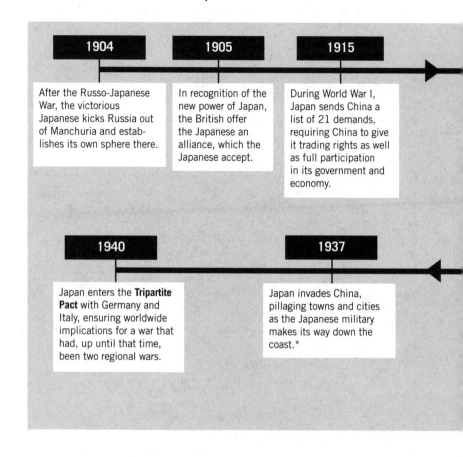

1904

After the Russo-Japanese War, the victorious Japanese kicks Russia out of Manchuria and establishes its own sphere there.

1905

In recognition of the new power of Japan, the British offer the Japanese an alliance, which the Japanese accept.

1915

During World War I, Japan sends China a list of 21 demands, requiring China to give it trading rights as well as full participation in its government and economy.

1940

Japan enters the **Tripartite Pact** with Germany and Italy, ensuring worldwide implications for a war that had, up until that time, been two regional wars.

1937

Japan invades China, pillaging towns and cities as the Japanese military makes its way down the coast.*

Japan's war with China (the one that began in 1937) merged into the global conflagration of World War II that later started to burn in Europe.

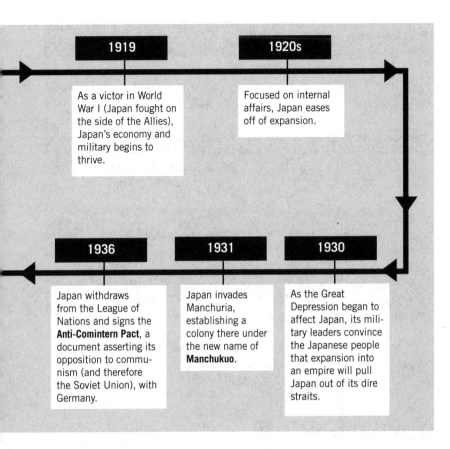

1919

As a victor in World War I (Japan fought on the side of the Allies), Japan's economy and military begins to thrive.

1920s

Focused on internal affairs, Japan eases off of expansion.

1936

Japan withdraws from the League of Nations and signs the **Anti-Comintern Pact**, a document asserting its opposition to communism (and therefore the Soviet Union), with Germany.

1931

Japan invades Manchuria, establishing a colony there under the new name of **Manchukuo**.

1930

As the Great Depression began to affect Japan, its military leaders convince the Japanese people that expansion into an empire will pull Japan out of its dire straits.

Responding to Japan's expansion into China, the United States froze Japanese assets and imposed sanctions. By 1941, Japan made war plans against the United States, and on December 7, 1941, the Japanese bombed a U.S. naval station in Hawaii at **Pearl Harbor**. The United States was stunned and promptly declared war against Japan. In response, Germany declared war against the United States.

A Study in Contrasts ❶

Nationalism in Europe and Japan	Nationalism in Their Colonies
Fueled by racism and fascism	Focused on self-determination
Synonymous with national expansion and conquest	Synonymous with the goal of sovereignty

Totalitarianism	Fascism
Rules absolutely, attempting to control every aspect of life	Rules as a kind of totalitarian; fascism is a subset of totalitarianism
Communist totalitarian leaders, such as Stalin are often referred to as extreme left-wing because they seek to destroy traditional institutions and class distinctions, even as they retain absolute power themselves.	Fascist rulers are often regarded as extremely right-wing because they rely on traditional institutions and social distinctions to enforce their rule (extremely nationalistic, often rooted in racism).

In their extreme forms, both left-wing (communist) and right-wing (fascist) governments use the same tactic: totalitarianism. In each case, all power rests in the hands of a single militaristic leader.

Back in Europe... ❶

Hitler's forces were devastating. Their war tactic, known as **blitzkrieg** ("lightning war"), destroyed everything it its path with historically unprecedented speed. The swiftly moving German forces acquired so much territory to the east of Poland that Stalin was forced to mobilize. Within 10 days, Germany and Russia had divided Poland between them. Hitler then focused on the western front, invading Holland and Belgium in early 1940. Two days later, German forces entered France on their way to controlling most of continental Europe.

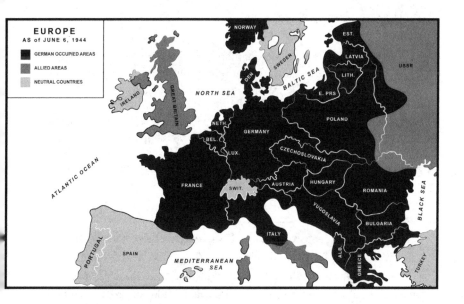

Allied Leaders

The Allies were led by Winston Churchill, Franklin Roosevelt, and Joseph Stalin (shown from left to right in the photo below). Roosevelt would die in April 1945 before the end of the war and be succeeded by **Harry Truman**. While the leaders had a common enemy in Nazi Germany, they had vastly different ideas about what Europe should look like after the war.

D-Day 💬

The Allies had a difficult time launching a land attack against the Germans because its resources were spread so thin—the Allies were busy fighting the Japanese in the Pacific, and they had their hands full with Germany and Italy in Africa. However, the tide began to turn in 1943 when the Allies took control of Italy. The following year, American, British, and Canadian forces stormed the French beaches of Normandy on **D-Day** (June 6, 1944). With the help of the French resistance, the Allies fought their way across northern France and liberated the country by the end of the summer.

💬 The scale of destruction in World War II was unprecedented. Mass casualties occurred due to new military technologies as well as the scale of the war. Besides the destruction left in Hiroshima and Nagasaki from the atomic bomb dropped by the United States, over 20,000 people died in the American and British bombing campaign of the German city of Dresden. Some military campaigns were even deadlier: when the Japanese invaded the Chinese capital of **Nanjing** in 1937, they left a trail of dead in the range of 40,000 to 300,000 unarmed Chinese. As horrifying as these events were, the number of dead pale in comparison to the **Holocaust**.

Holocaust ❗

Outside of Germany, few knew the full scale of the Nazi regime's atrocities after the war was over. In an ongoing slaughter known as the **Holocaust,** but known in Nazi Germany as "The Final Solution," millions of Jews who lived in Germany and German-occupied lands were rounded up, blamed for every problem in society, and methodically killed in gas chambers and firing lines, their bodies disposed of in ovens and mass graves.

Outcomes of the Holocaust
As many as 6 million Jews were killed.
As many as 6 million Poles, Slavs, Roma, homosexuals, disabled people, and political dissidents were killed.
Public support for the creation of a Jewish homeland—Israel—rose sharply.

After the War ❶

With the economies and infrastructure of European countries devastated following World War II, the United States was again in position to lend assistance—the U.S. had experienced a wartime economic surge and no damage to its infrastructure. The United States offered billions of dollars to the nations of Europe in order to help rebuild. The plan was known as the **Marshall Plan**, named after Secretary of State George C. Marshall, and offered to all European nations. For the most part, only Western European nations accepted. Greece and Turkey also accepted assistance, a strategic move for the United States, as allies in Eastern Europe would prove important during the Cold War.

A series of international organizations were also created to prevent such a war from breaking out again in the future:

- United Nations (UN)*
- World Bank
- International Monetary Fund (IMF)
- General Agreement on Trade and Tariffs (World Trade Organization, or WTO)

 Ask Yourself...

1. How was World War II a continuation of the First World War?
2. What factors led to the establishment of totalitarian governments?

The United Nations had more muscle than the failed League of Nations and had the goal of mediating international conflicts, with an option to intervene. The other organizations were created with the idea that if countries were financially connected, the chance of violent outbreaks would be reduced.

Communism and the Cold War

Although they were allies during World War II, the United States and the Soviet Union had vastly different worldviews. The United States was democratic and capitalist, while the Soviet Union was totalitarian and communist. Neither country wanted the other to spread its influence beyond its own borders, so even before the war had ended, each developed strategies to contain the other. This standoff would last for nearly 50 years.

The Cold War in Europe

Cold War Beginnings ❗

As World War II was winding down in February 1945, President Franklin D. Roosevelt, Winston Churchill, and Joseph Stalin met at Yalta in Crimea to discuss the postwar division of Europe. This was known as the **Yalta Conference.** Following the surrender of Germany and the death of Roosevelt, a similar meeting (with new U.S. President Truman taking the place of Roosevelt) took place in the German city of Potsdam. The leaders came to three agreements in what was known as the **Potsdam Agreement:**

❶ Germany would undergo democratization, denazification (trials for war criminals), demilitarization, decentralization, and decartelization (transition to a free-market economy)*.

❷ Japanese occupation of Indochina would see two parts of a Japanese surrender:
- Japanese soldiers north of a marker known as the 16th parallel would surrender to Communist China.
- Japanese soldiers south of the 16th parallel would surrender to the British.

❸ While the United States, Great Britain, and USSR agreed to let Poland create its own government, they soon recognized the Soviet Union's takeover of the Polish government. The Polish saw this as a "western betrayal."

It was during the meeting in Potsdam, weeks before the bombings of Hiroshima and Nagasaki, that President Truman first let Stalin know about an American super weapon, planting the seeds for a future arms race.

Demilitarization, decentralization, and decartelization meant major changes to the German economy: economic output would be spread out over competing businesses and would not involve any products that could be used for war. Goodbye steel production and ship building, hello toys and beer.

Truman Doctrine 💬

Determined to protect its borders and ideology, the Soviet Union demanded that its neighboring states, including Poland, Czechoslovakia, Hungary, Romania, and Bulgaria, be under its influence as well. The United States wanted those nations to have free elections, but the Soviet Union refused and simply set up puppet governments in those countries.

In response, the United States took a new, postwar approach to its foreign policy in 1947: the **Truman Doctrine**.

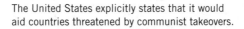

The United States explicitly states that it would aid countries threatened by communist takeovers.

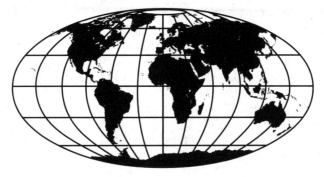

This policy is known as **containment**, as in "containing" your enemy.

Occupied Germany ❗

Based on the agreements at Yalta and Potsdam, Germany was divided into four regions, each under the influence of one of four Allies: France, Great Britain, the United States, and the Soviet Union. In 1948, the French, British, and U.S. regions merged into one, forming a democratic republic known as **West Germany**, while the Soviet Union's region became **East Germany**. Berlin, Germany's capital, was in the eastern side, the Soviet-occupied region.

Berlin Blockade and Airlift ❗

The fact that Berlin was located in East Germany presented a problem. The city, like Germany itself, was divided into eastern and western zones. However, the Soviets wanted all of Berlin to be under its control, so they cut off land access to Berlin from the west in an action known as the **Berlin Blockade.** The West retaliated by flying in food and fuel to the "trapped" western half of the city, which became known as the **Berlin Airlift.**

Eventually, the Soviets relented and Berlin was divided in half. In 1961, the Soviets built a wall between the two halves, preventing access to the West until the wall famously fell in 1989.

The Berlin Wall became a popular place for people to express their opinions about the political situation in Germany. Artists from around the world created graffiti art on the wall, shown here. The West Berlin side of the wall was completely covered, while the East Berlin side remained bare, as people were not allowed close enough to that side.

Soviet Bloc versus Western Bloc ❗

It was Winston Churchill who first called the imaginary line that ran through a divided Europe the **Iron Curtain**. The Iron Curtain separated the **Western Bloc** from the **Soviet Bloc**.

Western Bloc	Soviet (or Eastern) Bloc
Nations allied with the United States (Great Britain, France, West Germany, Canada, and many others)	Nations allied with the Soviet Union (Poland, East Germany, Romania, Hungary, and several others)
Formed a military alliance of mutual defense called NATO (North Atlantic Treaty Organization)	Responded to the formation of NATO by creating a military alliance known as the **Warsaw Pact**

Nuclear Proliferation ❗

For more than 40 years, NATO and the Warsaw Pact alliances loaded their borders with weapons—first conventional weapons and then nuclear weapons—and dared the other to strike first.

The **International Atomic Energy Agency (IAEA)**, the watchdog established in 1957, and the **Nuclear Nonproliferation Treaty** of 1968, attempted to limit nuclear technology to just five superpowers: China, Russia, the United States, Great Britain, and France. Still, weapons development continued even after the collapse of the Soviet Union.

The Cold War affected different countries in different ways, and the impact of communism extended beyond the Soviet Union and Europe to Asia and Latin America.

China: From Dynasty to Republic to Communism ❶

China experienced significant changes following the fall of the Manchu Dynasty in 1911. After a stint as a nationalist, more Westernized republic, China took a surprising turn toward communism.

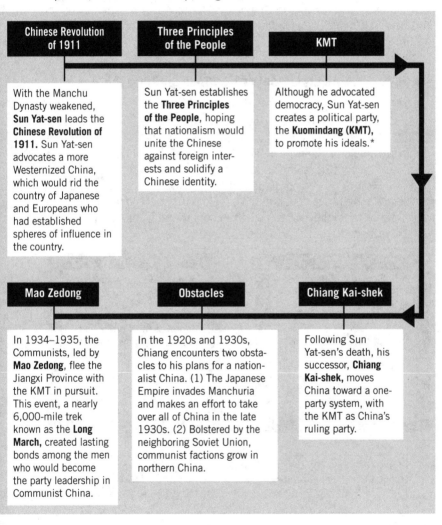

Chinese Revolution of 1911

With the Manchu Dynasty weakened, **Sun Yat-sen** leads the **Chinese Revolution of 1911.** Sun Yat-sen advocates a more Westernized China, which would rid the country of Japanese and Europeans who had established spheres of influence in the country.

Three Principles of the People

Sun Yat-sen establishes the **Three Principles of the People**, hoping that nationalism would unite the Chinese against foreign interests and solidify a Chinese identity.

KMT

Although he advocated democracy, Sun Yat-sen creates a political party, the **Kuomindang (KMT),** to promote his ideals.*

Mao Zedong

In 1934–1935, the Communists, led by **Mao Zedong,** flee the Jiangxi Province with the KMT in pursuit. This event, a nearly 6,000-mile trek known as the **Long March,** created lasting bonds among the men who would become the party leadership in Communist China.

Obstacles

In the 1920s and 1930s, Chiang encounters two obstacles to his plans for a nationalist China. (1) The Japanese Empire invades Manchuria and makes an effort to take over all of China in the late 1930s. (2) Bolstered by the neighboring Soviet Union, communist factions grow in northern China.

Chiang Kai-shek

Following Sun Yat-sen's death, his successor, **Chiang Kai-shek,** moves China toward a one-party system, with the KMT as China's ruling party.

While he did not believe in redistributing wealth, Sun Yat-sen did aim to improve economic output with socialism—using the government to finance industry.

The KMT's army and the Communist Party's Red Army spent World War II fighting one another while also uniting to fight against the Japanese. The United States gave financial support to the KMT, though the Soviets were less generous in support of the Red Army (partly due to their focus on Germany). This initially led to a lopsided civil war.

As in other parts of the world, the end of World War II resulted in power vacuums that resulted in a clash between democracy and communism in China.

Republic of China and People's Republic of China

In 1949, Mao Zedong led millions of peasants from northern China to defeat the KMT. The KMT retreated to Taiwan, establishing the **Republic of China**. The communists on mainland China renamed the country the **People's Republic of China**. Under the leadership of Mao, the People's Republic of China became the largest communist nation in the world. China and Taiwan diverged significantly following the establishment of the People's Republic of China. While China benefited in many ways from its alliances, Taiwan gained the economic advantage in the long term. See the graphic below.

Republic of China	People's Republic of China
+ Developed into an economic powerhouse	+ Maintained a strategic military alliance with one of the world's two strongest powers—the USSR
− Lost credibility when the United Nations and the United States eventually recognized the People's Republic as the true China	− Struggled economically in comparison to Taiwan

Taiwan has rejected China's efforts toward reunification, but the two nations have grown close together, especially as the economies of both nations grew stronger in the latter part of the 20th century.

Key People: Mao Zedong

- Inspired by Stalin's five-year plans, Mao collectivized agriculture and industry with successful results.
- The success of Mao's five-year plans was erased by the Great Leap Forward.
  - To accelerate economic productivity, Mao delegated unrealistic production goals to China's Communes.
  - Unable to achieve these goals, local officials lied about their economic output, causing widespread starvation. As a result, 30 million people died.
- China lost the financial support of the Soviet Union, which wanted the entire world to become communist and under its control—a concession Mao would not make.

Cultural Revolution 🛈

Without Soviet support, Mao knew that he needed to modernize his military, so he stepped away from controlling the economy to work toward that goal. While he was away, moderate reformers allowed some elements of capitalism to enter society, leading to some economic success. In fact, the results even helped modernize China's military: China tested its first atomic bomb in 1964. However, Mao was disappointed that the country had veered from its Marxist aims. In response, he instituted the **Cultural Revolution** in 1966.

Cultural Revolution in Theory	• Mao sought to do away with anything resembling a privileged ruling class. • Goverment was to erase evidence of Western-influenced intellegensia.	Cultural Revolution in Practice	• Universities shut down for four years; doctors, lawyers, and artists were sent to collective farms for "cultural retraining." • Political dissidents were imprisoned or killed
Cultural Revolution Impact	• Universities taught communist studies and vocational training. • Mao's Little Red Book, a collection of his teachings, became a symbol of the forced egalitarianism.	Cultural Revolution Results	• The plan failed to advance China economically or socially. • China realized it needed to open itself to Western ideas.

Note the Change: From Dynastic China to Communist China

For nearly 2,000 years, Confucianism and a class-based social structure dominated China. The Communist Revolution all but erased this class-based system, along with the traditional value placed on large families both out of economic necessity and Confucian belief.

China Looks West (Sort of)

In 1976, the new leadership under **Deng Xiaoping** began to focus on restructuring its economic policies. What was once a total command economy began to allow some free-market capitalist components, including some private ownership and entrepreneurialism. The results were largely positive, as the Chinese economy made a dramatic turn-around in the 1970s and has for the most part sustained this growth until today.

Despite these economic reforms, the Chinese government remains politically similar to totalitarian communist regimes, as evidenced by the **Tiananmen Square massacre**. In the post-Mao era, students and other dissenters had congregated from time to time at Tiananmen Square in Beijing to advocate for democratic reform. In one such event in 1989, the government opened fire on protesters, killing hundreds.

Cold War in Asia 🔴

The Cold War's impact on Asia did not stop with China. When Japan surrendered, both Korea and **Indochina** (modern-day Vietnam), countries that were occupied by Imperial Japan, saw a Germany-like division between communist regions and democratic, free-market regions, resulting in military conflict. See the following table.

Country	Korea	Indochina (Vietnam)
Division	38th parallel	17th parallel
Supporters	• Soviet Union in the North, United States in the South • Two separate governments were established in 1948.	• China in the North, France and United States in the South • An agreement to divide was signed in 1954 in Geneva following an uprising by communist rebels, the **Vietminh**, against their French colonizers.
Reason for Military Conflict	The superpower occupiers withdrew troops in 1949. In 1950, North Korea invaded South Korea in an attempt to to create one Korea under a communist government. The UN condemned the attack, and the U.S. and U.K. led a multinational force to push back the North Koreans.	**Ho Chi Minh**, who led the communists in the North, aimed to reunify Vietnam as a communist state. Ho Chi Minh supported communist guerillas in the South, and South Vietnamese leader **Ngo Dihn Diem** fought back, leading to a war between the two sides.

Country	Korea	Indochina (Vietnam)
The Conflict	The United States made tremendous headway and, under the leadership of **General MacArthur,** nearly entered China. However, just as North Korea looked defeated, China entered the fray and battled the U.S. and U.K. along the 38th parallel.	The United States and France came to South Vietnam's aid but were unable to get any footing in North Vietnam, often outmaneuvered in the dense rainforest by the North Vietnamese arm, the **Viet Cong**. The U.S. eventually withdrew its troops in 1975.
Outcome	An armistice was signed in 1953 to cease the fighting between North Korea and South Korea. South Korea went on to become an economic power, while North Korea, through isolationist policies, nutty rulers, and massive food shortages, has floundered, though not without creating a large military with nuclear weapon technology.	South Vietnam eventually fell to the North, and a peace treaty led to the unification of Vietnam as a communist nation. The United States viewed the war in Vietnam largely as a failure of its foreign policy.

Cold War in Latin America 🗎

During the Cold War, Latin American nations were still developing economically and thus became playing fields for U.S. influence. The most significant shot fired was in Cuba, which had been a U.S. protectorate under the Platt Amendment since the end of the Spanish-American War. The United States invested in Cuban businesses and plantations, but these investments often enriched the wealthy and left the poor behind. Class resentment grew, which made the political climate ripe for a communist revolution.

Tensions came to a head when the U.S.-supported **Batista Dictatorship** (1939–1959) fell to a peasant revolt under the leadership of **Fidel Castro.** The revolution was hailed as a great success against a dictator, and Fidel Castro, supposedly the great promoter of democracy, took control of the government, suspended plans for an election, and established a communist dictatorship.

From the Bay of Pigs Invasion to the Cuban Missile Crisis

The United States trained a group of anti-Castro Cuban exiles living in the United States, convinced that an invasion by these exiles would lead to a popular revolt against Castro. It didn't work out that way. In 1961, President Kennedy authorized the **Bay of Pigs Invasion,** but with only the small force of Cuban exiles, who were quickly captured after they landed.

In 1962, U.S. spy planes detected Soviet missiles in Cuba. To prevent further shipments from the Soviet Union, President Kennedy immediately established a naval blockade around Cuba. This resulted in a three-week standoff known as the **Cuban Missile Crisis.**

Latin America Experiments with New Political Systems

The **export economies** of Latin American countries (a reliance on coffee, fruit, sugar, and oil) have long made them susceptible to debt and weak domestic economies. This created some instability in the 20th century, and various countries experimented with new economic and political systems.

Since Franklin D. Roosevelt's administration, the United States had maintained a noninterventionist **"Good Neighbor Policy"** toward Latin America. However, after two world wars and the Great Depression, that region became less of a priority for the United States. Its decreased presence in Latin America allowed individual nations to shape their own destinies, which sometimes meant looking toward communism.

The types of governments pursued by Latin American countries fell into three main categories:

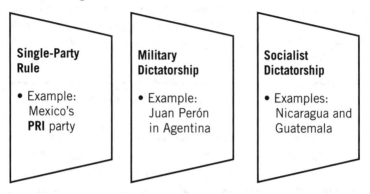

Single-Party Rule

- Example: Mexico's **PRI** party

Military Dictatorship

- Example: Juan Perón in Agentina

Socialist Dictatorship

- Examples: Nicaragua and Guatemala

Nicaragua and El Salvador 💬

During the Cold War, the United States rekindled its interest in Latin America, often intervening to stave off the influences of communism, per its containment policy. Of most interest to the United States was the emergence of social democracies in countries like Nicaragua and Guatemala. Nicaragua was used as a staging ground during the Bay of Pigs Invasion, and later during the 1980s, the United States backed (and trained, via the CIA) forces to resist the **Sandinista** guerrillas, a socialist-liberation party attempting revolutions in Latin America.

Democracy and Mexico ❶

The **Mexican Revolution** began in 1910, following the unpopular presidency of Porfirio Díaz. The revolution gave rise to a constitution in 1917 that established a single-party system in Mexico. However, alternate parties were finally allowed to participate in elections beginning in 2000. In that election, the opposing party, the **PAN (National Action Party)** won the presidency, and then won again in the 2006 election, though the PRI candidate won the presidential election in 2012.

Fall of Communism in Eastern Europe ❗

During the Cold War, the standard of living in Western Europe significantly outpaced that of Eastern Europe. The growing divide between the "rich" West and the "poor" East became obvious to those living behind the Iron Curtain, and revolts were inevitable. Revolt against Soviet control was not just about economics; a variety of nationalities lived in the Eastern bloc, and they wanted to control their own destiny through democratic and economic reforms.

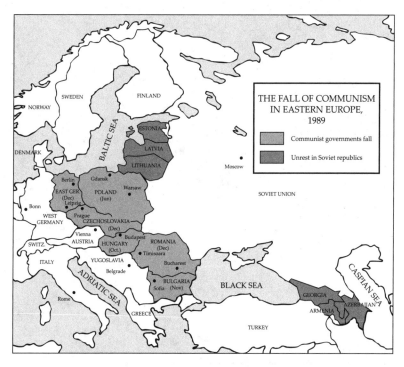

The Fall of Communism in Eastern Europe

Unification of Germany 💬

After more than 40 years as a divided nation, Germany was reunified in 1989. Despite concerns over how a unified Germany might function after being at the center of two world wars, East Germany's genuine desire for economic reform, political freedom, and an improved standard of living outweighed those concerns. Here are some key events that led to unification.

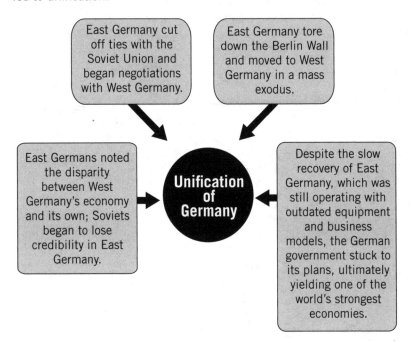

East Germany cut off ties with the Soviet Union and began negotiations with West Germany.

East Germany tore down the Berlin Wall and moved to West Germany in a mass exodus.

East Germans noted the disparity between West Germany's economy and its own; Soviets began to lose credibility in East Germany.

Unification of Germany

Despite the slow recovery of East Germany, which was still operating with outdated equipment and business models, the German government stuck to its plans, ultimately yielding one of the world's strongest economies.

Soviet Union Breaks Apart ❗

The ascension of **Mikhail Gorbachev** to power in 1985 signaled the beginning of the end of the Soviet Union. His policies, including *glasnost* (openness) resembled Western economies more than a communist state.

With nuclear arms treaties signed with the United States, private enterprises popping up around the country, and a reevaluation of the darker parts of Soviet history, Gorbachev's tenure saw the Cold War come to an end. In 1991, the Soviet Union disintegrated (relatively peacefully) into numerous independent countries—including the Soviet Union's return to plain old Russia.

A New Russian Democracy 💬

Under **Boris Yeltsen**, Russia's first president, the country attempted to reform its economy, government, and trade in accordance with its 1993 constitution. Frustrated with the slow pace of reform and the corruption evident from former Soviet officials trying to enrich themselves under the rules, Yeltsen resigned in 1999.

Following Yeltsen's presidency, former **KGB** (Soviet security) agent **Vladimir Putin** won the presidency twice. Putin's brand of "democracy" has been highly corrupt and authoritarian, in his blocking of opposition candidates and crackdown on the free press, among other abuses of power.

Poland Rejects Soviet Control 💬

The decline of communism brought sweeping reform to Poland and its government, which had been trying for years to prevent the spread of anticommunist sentiment.

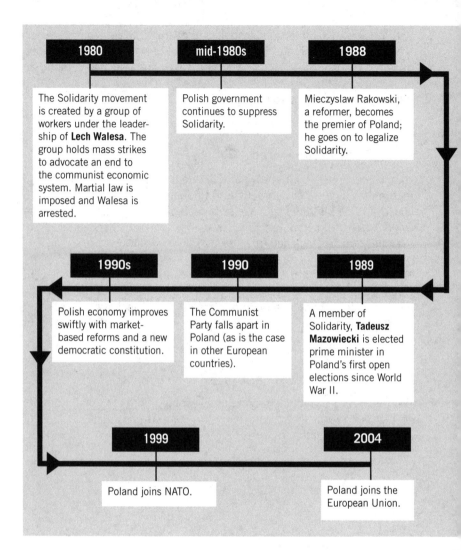

1980

The Solidarity movement is created by a group of workers under the leadership of **Lech Walesa**. The group holds mass strikes to advocate an end to the communist economic system. Martial law is imposed and Walesa is arrested.

mid-1980s

Polish government continues to suppress Solidarity.

1988

Mieczyslaw Rakowski, a reformer, becomes the premier of Poland; he goes on to legalize Solidarity.

1990s

Polish economy improves swiftly with market-based reforms and a new democratic constitution.

1990

The Communist Party falls apart in Poland (as is the case in other European countries).

1989

A member of Solidarity, **Tadeusz Mazowiecki** is elected prime minister in Poland's first open elections since World War II.

1999

Poland joins NATO.

2004

Poland joins the European Union.

End of the Cold War ❗

The end of the Cold War was not entirely peaceful. Two notable cases are the Balkans and Chechnya.

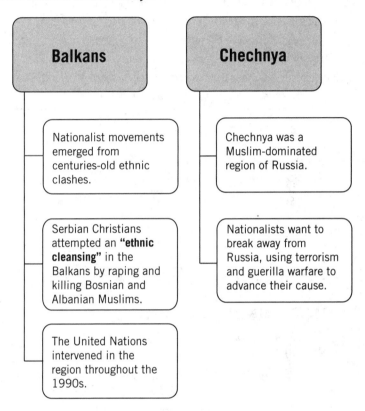

Balkans

Nationalist movements emerged from centuries-old ethnic clashes.

Serbian Christians attempted an **"ethnic cleansing"** in the Balkans by raping and killing Bosnian and Albanian Muslims.

The United Nations intervened in the region throughout the 1990s.

Chechnya

Chechnya was a Muslim-dominated region of Russia.

Nationalists want to break away from Russia, using terrorism and guerilla warfare to advance their cause.

During the Cold War, the terms "West" and "East" were frequently used to describe much of the world, especially the northern hemisphere. The West, led by the United States, was generally democratic, capitalist, and prosperous; the East, led by the Soviet Union, was communist and generally totalitarian as well as less prosperous in terms of per capita standard of living. After the fall of communism in most of the world in the early 1990s, these terms began to lose their relevance.

 Ask Yourself...

1. How did the Cold War reorder international alliances?
2. What challenges did countries that adopted communism encounter?

Independence Movements and Developments in Asia and Africa

A wave of independence movements in the post–World War II era marked the beginning of the end of European imperialism. During the Cold War, as the United States and Western Europe defended people's right to choose their own futures (self-determination) under democratic systems, it became difficult for colonial powers to reconcile their post–World War II principles with their imperialist policies. More importantly, it was increasingly difficult for subjugated peoples to tolerate their treatment, so they rose up and demanded independence.

Indian Independence ❗

The Indian struggle for independence from Great Britain started slowly, and then accelerated following the massacre of unarmed protesters by British officials. While the movement eventually succeeded in a mostly nonviolent way, it was marred by violence between Hindu and Muslim extremists.

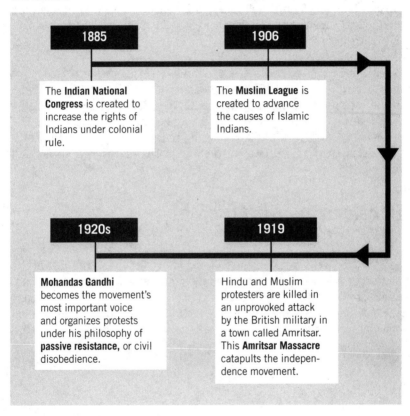

1885

The **Indian National Congress** is created to increase the rights of Indians under colonial rule.

1906

The **Muslim League** is created to advance the causes of Islamic Indians.

1920s

Mohandas Gandhi becomes the movement's most important voice and organizes protests under his philosophy of **passive resistance,** or civil disobedience.

1919

Hindu and Muslim protesters are killed in an unprovoked attack by the British military in a town called Amritsar. This **Amritsar Massacre** catapults the independence movement.

While both Hindus and Muslims worked together for independence, radical members from each group found it difficult to tolerate one another. Gandhi, who was raised Hindu but believed in mutual respect among different religious groups, called for Indian unity above religious considerations.

The Muslim League, meanwhile, actively pushed for the creation of a Muslim nation. When Britain granted independence to India following World War II, **Muhammad Ali Jinnah** pressed for a separate Muslim nation in the northern Islamic regions.

When the British turned the subcontinent over to the new leaders of independent India in 1947, it separated the country into thirds: India in the south and Pakistan in two parts. The northwest portion became Pakistan, and the portion to the east is modern-day Bangladesh. The result was chaotic, with millions fleeing to the country where their religion (Islam or Hinduism) was dominant. Today, the two nations are still fighting.

Decolonization in Africa 🔋

After World War II, African nations also began to assert their independence. They were partly inspired by events in India and the rest of the world, but they were also motivated by the war itself. Hundreds of thousands of Africans fought for their colonial powers during the war; many felt that if they were willing to die for their governing countries, then they had earned the right to live free.

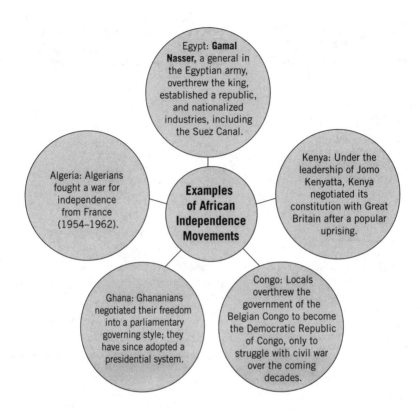

Egypt: **Gamal Nasser,** a general in the Egyptian army, overthrew the king, established a republic, and nationalized industries, including the Suez Canal.

Algeria: Algerians fought a war for independence from France (1954–1962).

Examples of African Independence Movements

Kenya: Under the leadership of Jomo Kenyatta, Kenya negotiated its constitution with Great Britain after a popular uprising.

Ghana: Ghananians negotiated their freedom into a parliamentary governing style; they have since adopted a presidential system.

Congo: Locals overthrew the government of the Belgian Congo to become the Democratic Republic of Congo, only to struggle with civil war over the coming decades.

South African Independence ❗

South Africa became a significant British colony complete with extensive investment in infrastructure and institutions. In 1910, the colony established its own constitution to become the Union of South Africa. It was still part of the British Commonwealth but now exercised a considerable amount of self-rule.

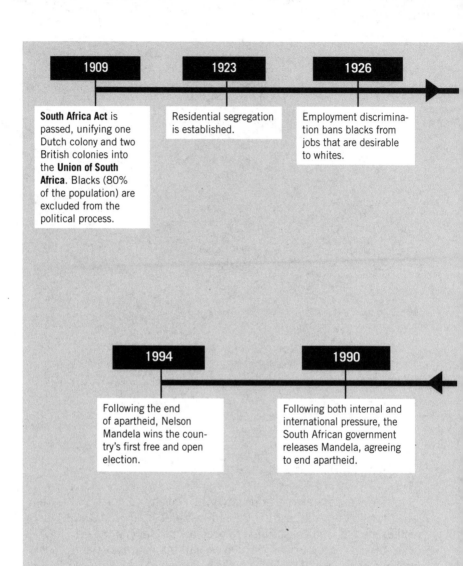

1909

South Africa Act is passed, unifying one Dutch colony and two British colonies into the **Union of South Africa**. Blacks (80% of the population) are excluded from the political process.

1923

Residential segregation is established.

1926

Employment discrimination bans blacks from jobs that are desirable to whites.

1994

Following the end of apartheid, Nelson Mandela wins the country's first free and open election.

1990

Following both internal and international pressure, the South African government releases Mandela, agreeing to end apartheid.

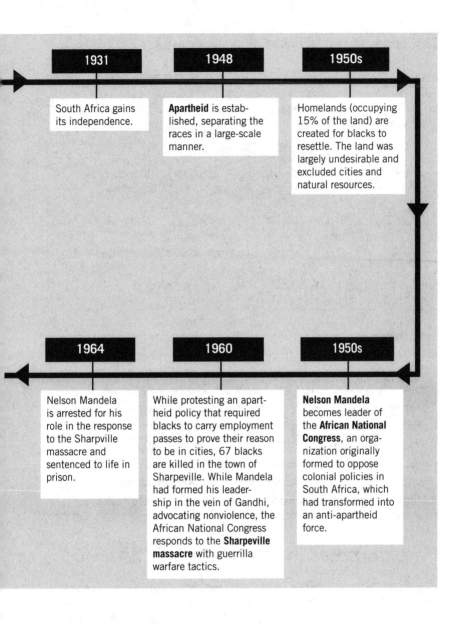

1931

South Africa gains its independence.

1948

Apartheid is established, separating the races in a large-scale manner.

1950s

Homelands (occupying 15% of the land) are created for blacks to resettle. The land was largely undesirable and excluded cities and natural resources.

1964

Nelson Mandela is arrested for his role in the response to the Sharpville massacre and sentenced to life in prison.

1960

While protesting an apartheid policy that required blacks to carry employment passes to prove their reason to be in cities, 67 blacks are killed in the town of Sharpeville. While Mandela had formed his leadership in the vein of Gandhi, advocating nonviolence, the African National Congress responds to the **Sharpeville massacre** with guerrilla warfare tactics.

1950s

Nelson Mandela becomes leader of the **African National Congress**, an organization originally formed to oppose colonial policies in South Africa, which had transformed into an anti-apartheid force.

Challenges Faced by Post-Colonial Africa ❗

In 1963, nations across Africa formed the **Organization of African Unity (OAU)** in order to promote African solidarity and resist colonialism. In 2001, the OAU was replaced by the **African Union**. Its mission of promoting peace and stability in Africa has met numerous challenges:

- Civil wars have been ongoing in member nations such as Chad, Sudan, Somalia, Rwanda, and the Democratic Republic of Congo.
- "Big man" politics, corruption, and military coups have thwarted attempts at democracy throughout Africa.
- Crippling debt owed to the International Monetary Fund (IMF) and the World Bank has hampered the ability of member nations to see real economic growth.

Compare Them: Independence in Africa and India

Both India and Africa successfully gained independence in the years following World War II, and both were subsequently torn apart by ethnic and religious strife. The tensions between Hindus and Muslims in India, which existed before the country's colonization, reemerged as the British departed. In many African nations, independence caused long-held tribal hatreds to resurface in power struggles. Even after generations of colonial rule, Africans remembered old rivalries and frequently acted on them.

Decolonization in the Middle East ❗

After the fall of the Ottoman Empire and the creation of modern-day Turkey at the close of World War I, the Middle East, which was largely comprised of old Ottoman lands, was temporarily put under control of the League of Nations. France oversaw Syria and Lebanon, and Great Britain oversaw Palestine, Jordan, and Iraq. Persia (Iran) had been carved up into British and Russian spheres of influence since the 19th century. The remainder of the Middle East, Arabia, united into a Saudi kingdom following the fall of the Ottoman Empire.

The Creation of Israel ⚠

Promised Land

- At the time of the Roman Empire, the Hebrews (Jews) occupied land in Palestine.
- Through a series of conquests, Jews largely fled the region.
- Most Jews migrated to Europe, though still saw Palestine as the biblical "Promised Land."

Palestinians

- While some Jews remained, the Arabic population of Palestine eventually became Islamic, and for many generations, Palestinian Muslims called Palestine home.

Balfour

- **Zionists** (Jewish nationalists) in Great Britain convinced British foreign secretary Arthur Balfour to create a Jewish homeland in Palestine.
- In 1917, the **Balfour Declaration** declared a right for the Jewish people to have a homeland in Palestine.

Jewish Settlement

- Since the British controlled Palestine following World War I, Jewish settlement in Palestine was an achievable goal.
- By World War II, 500,000 Jews emigrated to Palestine from both Russia and Germany.
- **Pogroms** (anti-Semetic mobs) popped up in Russia, not just in Nazi-occupied regions of Europe.

Israel

- The United Nations (which replaced the ineffectual League of Nations) official created two Palestines in 1948: one for Jews and the other for Muslims (Palestinians).
- **David Ben-Gurion** became Israel's first prime minister.

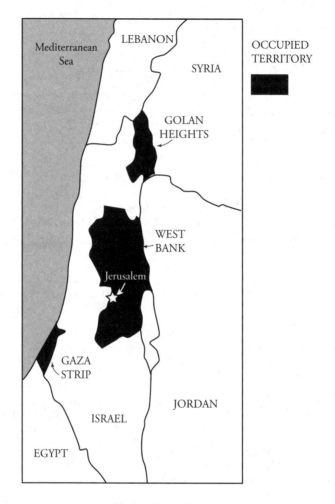

Modern Israel

Conflicts in the Middle East ❗

Immediately after the establishment of the state of Israel, Muslims from six Arab countries attacked Israel in what became known as the **1948 Arab-Israeli War.** But the Israelis shocked and awed them with their quick organization and military capability. Within months, the Israelis controlled most of Palestine, including the Palestinian sections, while

Jordan held the remaining portions. Suddenly, Palestinians had no land to call their own.

Six-Day War 💬

As Jews flocked to Israel from all over the world, skirmishes continued between Israel and Arab countries, including 1967's **Six-Day War**, in which Israel gained more land:

- Gaza Strip (from Egypt)
- Golan Heights (from Syria)
- West Bank (from Jordan), which included the historical Jewish homeland: the city of Jerusalem

Attempts at Peace ❗

Muslims throughout the region resented Israeli control of Jerusalem because the city housed the Dome of the Rock, a revered Islamic shrine. The territorial gains resulted in new waves of Palestinian refugees to Jerusalem. In 1978, Egypt and Israel agreed to peace talks and traveled to the United States to sign the **Camp David Accords.**

- **The Players**: Israeli Prime Minister **Menachem Begin**, Egyptian President **Anwar Sadat**
- **The Meeting:** While the two men initially met with each other on day one, the remaining 12 days consisted of U.S. President **Jimmy Carter** serving as an intermediary.
- **The Aftermath:** Sadat was assassinated in 1981. The lands Israel won in the Six-Day War remain highly contested.

Camp David Accords

- Peace established between Israel and Egypt.
- Israel withdraws from the West Bank and Gaza.
- Israel pulls out of the Sinai region of Egypt.
- Egypt recognizes Israel's right to exist.

Palestinian Liberation Organization ❗

In the years since the Camp David Accords, the Israelis and the Palestinians have been fighting over the Israeli occupation of the West Bank, Golan Heights, and Gaza Strip. The **Palestine Liberation Organization (PLO)**, a group dedicated to reclaiming the land and establishing a Palestinian state, has so far been unsuccessful in negotiating a homeland.

Barriers to Peace ➋

- **intifada*:** An uprising movement that has used terrorism against Israeli citizens in order to force Israel's withdrawal from disputed lands
- **Yassir Arafat:** Former PLO leader blamed for blocking the UN-backed "Roadmap to Peace"
- **Hamas:** A Palestinian liberation group that, along with **Hezbollah**, a militant Shia group, continued fighting with Israel into the 2000s

Iranian Revolution ❗

Reza Shah Pahlavi rose to power in 1925 by ousting the then-ruling shah, who had allowed Persia to fall under European spheres of influence.

Reza Shah attempted to defeat the European influence by modernizing. Ironically, to the shah, this meant Westernizing:

- Land reform
- Education reform
- Voting rights for women
- Educational and career opportunities for women
- Western dress for women

The modernization offended Islamic fundamentalists who wanted to make the teachings of the Qur'an the law of the land.

- The shah also was opposed by those who felt his reforms were not democratic enough.
- President Carter's visit to congratulate Iran on its modernization programs was the straw that broke the camel's back and led to the Iranian Revolution in 1979.

Following Arafat's death, **Mahmoud Abbas** was elected and quickly signed a ceasefire with Israel to end the intifada that began in 2000.

The Iranian Revolution turned Iran into a theocracy based on a strict, Shia interpretation of Islam.

- Ayatollah Khomeini led the revolution.
- Women were required to wear traditional Islamic clothing and fulfill traditional roles.

Iran-Iraq War (1980–1988) ❶

Iraq invaded Iran following a series of border disputes between the two countries. The United States quietly backed Iraq due to Iran taking U.S. hostages in 1979. Neither side took much land before a ceasefire was signed in 1988.

Since Ayatollah Khomeini's death in 1989, Iran has been characterized by a power struggle between powerful Islamic fundamentalist clerics and an increasingly vocal, reform-minded, and somewhat pro-Western majority. From 2005 to 2013, Tehran's ultra-conservative former mayor, **Mahmoud Ahmandinejad,** was president of Iran. He was succeeded by the more politically moderate leader Hassan Rouhani.

Oil Production in the Middle East ❶

The Industrial Revolution brought the world's attention to the Middle East. What appeared merely as goo before the Industrial Revolution turned out to be a useful natural resource to power industry and automobiles: oil.

The Middle East sits on two-thirds of the world's oil reserves. As a result, billions of dollars in annual revenue went to Saudi Arabia, Kuwait, Iran, and Iraq. In 1960, oil-producing nations realized the enormous influence they held and created **OPEC (Organization of Petroleum Exporting Countries),** a petroleum cartel.

Human Rights ❶

Colonies fought for liberation in the 20th century, and their struggles, along with the atrocities of the world wars, led to greater recognition of the concept of human rights.

Armenian Genocide, 1915–1923
Ottoman Turks exterminated 1.5 million Armenians as part of an ethnic cleansing known as the Armenian Genocide.

Cambodian Genocide, 1975–1979
The Khmer Rouge government killed as many as 3 million Cambodians who were considered political or ethnic enemies.

Rwandan Genocide, 1994
The Rwandan Genocide saw the ethnic majority of Rwanda (the Hutu) kill 800,000 (70–80%) of the ethnic minority (Tutsi) between April and July 1994.

The new focus on human rights in the 20th century played out in various forms of resistance such as art, popular protest, and self-sacrifice.

- **Art** Pablo Picasso painted *Guernica* to portray the horrors of the Spanish Civil War after Nazi and Italian planes aided Spanish dictator Francisco Franco by bombing the town of Guernica in 1937.
- **Protest and Activism** During the 1970s and 1980s, antiwar activists and environmentalists lodged a series of protests against nuclear weapons and what they considered unsafe nuclear energy sources.
- **Self-Sacrifice** In the 1960s and 1970s, Buddhist monks in Vietnam gave their lives to protest the Vietnam War when they self-immolated (set themselves on fire) in order to bring attention to the injustices of the war.

Human rights activists also brought greater attention to new philosophies and challenged assumptions about issues such as race and gender.

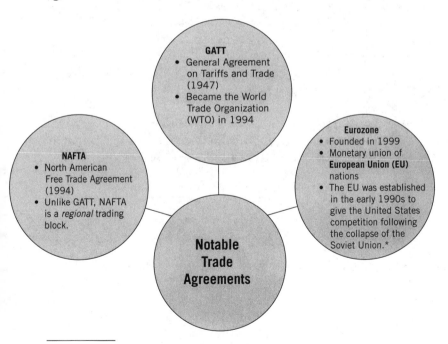

Ask Yourself...

1. What new conflicts arose from the process of post–World War II decolonization in different parts of the world?
2. How did decolonization influence a new understanding of human rights?

Globalization and the World Since 1980 ❗

Open Trade ❗

One of the aims of globalization is to make trade more open throughout the world by removing trade barriers such as tariffs. After World War II, trade agreements like **GATT**, **NAFTA**, and the **Eurozone** formed to do just that.

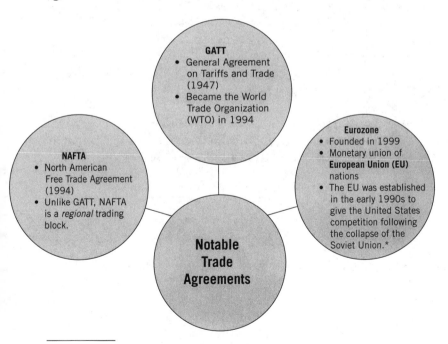

GATT
- General Agreement on Tariffs and Trade (1947)
- Became the World Trade Organization (WTO) in 1994

Eurozone
- Founded in 1999
- Monetary union of **European Union (EU)** nations
- The EU was established in the early 1990s to give the United States competition following the collapse of the Soviet Union.*

NAFTA
- North American Free Trade Agreement (1994)
- Unlike GATT, NAFTA is a *regional* trading block.

Notable Trade Agreements

Following the collapse of the USSR, the United States was the unchallenged superpower of the world. European nations seized the opportunity to give US markets some competition by banning together to create their own kind of economy of scale.

Even in the post-colonial era, globalism has led to Latin American nations experiencing a phenomenon known as **neocolonialism,** the use of economic and cultural pressure to influence culture and policy in developing nations.

China's Open Trade 💬

Since Deng Xiaoping flirted with capitalism in the 1970s, China has grown to become an industrial and economic juggernaut.

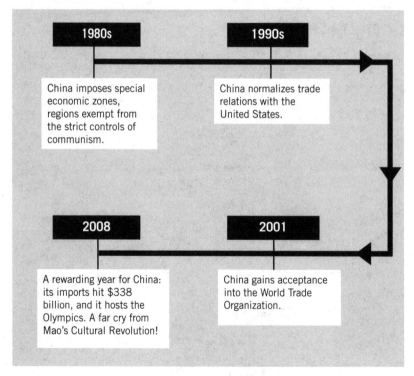

1980s

China imposes special economic zones, regions exempt from the strict controls of communism.

1990s

China normalizes trade relations with the United States.

2008

A rewarding year for China: its imports hit $338 billion, and it hosts the Olympics. A far cry from Mao's Cultural Revolution!

2001

China gains acceptance into the World Trade Organization.

Group of 6 💬

One economic organization of note is the **Group of Six** (**G6**), which was created in 1975 as a forum for the world's major industrialized democracies. The group has grown and shrunk over time, adding and subtracting members. Currently it meets annually to discuss issues of mutual or global concern, such as climate change, terrorism, and trade.

G6 Members	**G8 Members**
• United States	• United States
• Great Britain	• Great Britain
• West Germany (today, Germany)	• West Germany (today, Germany)
• Italy	• Italy
• Japan	• Japan
• France	• France
	• Canada (joined 1977)
	• Russia (joined 1997)*

After Russia invaded Ukraine in the 2014 Crimea Crisis, the group excluded Russia and currently meets as the G7 group of nations. In addition, a group of 19 nations plus EU representatives meets to represent both industrialized and developing countries as the **G20,** or the Group of 20 Finance Ministers and Central Bank Governors.

Other International Trade Agreements

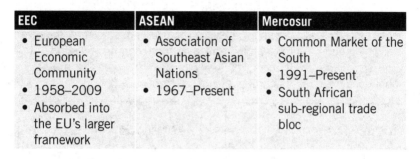

EEC	ASEAN	Mercosur
• European Economic Community • 1958–2009 • Absorbed into the EU's larger framework	• Association of Southeast Asian Nations • 1967–Present	• Common Market of the South • 1991–Present • South African sub-regional trade bloc

---

Note the Change: The Threat of "McDonaldization"

Consider for a moment just how far and wide fast food culture has spread since the first McDonald's restaurant opened in California in the late 1930s. Now there are McDonald's restaurants all over the world. The so-called "McDonaldization" of the world is both an example of and a metaphor for the spread of western popular culture to the rest of the world. Many countries, such as India and China, have embraced parts of western culture; other groups have rejected this "invasion" of modern western culture, which they see as a threat to their traditional ways.

War in Iraq 🛑

Globalization also has increased interest in maintaining international security. Iraq's move to overtake Kuwait's oil supply in 1990 set into motion a decades-long conflict in which the international community attempted to stabilize the region.

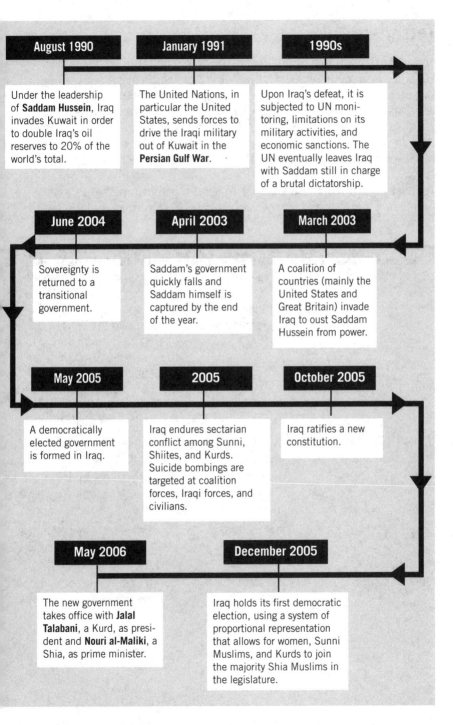

August 1990

Under the leadership of **Saddam Hussein**, Iraq invades Kuwait in order to double Iraq's oil reserves to 20% of the world's total.

January 1991

The United Nations, in particular the United States, sends forces to drive the Iraqi military out of Kuwait in the **Persian Gulf War**.

1990s

Upon Iraq's defeat, it is subjected to UN monitoring, limitations on its military activities, and economic sanctions. The UN eventually leaves Iraq with Saddam still in charge of a brutal dictatorship.

June 2004

Sovereignty is returned to a transitional government.

April 2003

Saddam's government quickly falls and Saddam himself is captured by the end of the year.

March 2003

A coalition of countries (mainly the United States and Great Britain) invade Iraq to oust Saddam Hussein from power.

May 2005

A democratically elected government is formed in Iraq.

2005

Iraq endures sectarian conflict among Sunni, Shiites, and Kurds. Suicide bombings are targeted at coalition forces, Iraqi forces, and civilians.

October 2005

Iraq ratifies a new constitution.

May 2006

The new government takes office with **Jalal Talabani**, a Kurd, as president and **Nouri al-Maliki**, a Shia, as prime minister.

December 2005

Iraq holds its first democratic election, using a system of proportional representation that allows for women, Sunni Muslims, and Kurds to join the majority Shia Muslims in the legislature.

Terrorism �",

The shrinking of the world due to globalization also threatened to suppress local cultures. Some living in developing nations undergoing the process of Westernization resented the lack of cultural orthodoxy and blamed the West for their country's rapid modernization. When this worldview was adopted by political extremists living in Islamic lands (people who had already held angst that their homeland had been occupied by western militaries), they saw the appeal of terrorist organizations.

Terrorist organizations use violence to send a political message. Some well-known terrorist acts at the dawn of the 21st century include the following.

Date	Location	Details
September 11, 2001	United States: New York City, Washington D.C., and Pennsylvania	Al Qeada operatives managed to take control of four American passenger jets and fly two of them into the **World Trade Center** in New York, one into the Pentagon in Washington, D.C., and one (presumably unintentionally) into a field in Pennsylvania. The death total reached nearly 3,000.
March 11, 2004	Spain: Madrid	The bombing of a commuter train killed 192 people.
February 14, 2005	Lebanon: Beirut	Coordinated bombings killed 22 people, including Lebanese Prime Minister Rafiq Hariri.
July 7, 2005	Great Britain: London	Coordinated bombings on the London subway system killed 53 people.
July 11, 2006	India: Mumbai	Seven bombs on the Mumbai Rail system killed 209 people.

Al Qaeda ❗

A terrorist group known as Al Qaeda carried out the September 11, 2001 attacks in the United States. The group was led at the time by **Osama bin Laden**, a wealthy construction heir who became radicalized and planned a series of attacks against the United States and other Western interests. Bin Laden offered three reasons for the attacks:

- The United States supports Israel.
- U.S. troops were stationed in Saudi Arabia, which is considered sacred land in Islam.
- The United States is the primary agent of globalization, which Al Qaeda believes is infecting Islamic culture.

The Taliban ❗

Immediately following the attacks of September 11, 2001, the United States launched a war on terrorism, targeting Al Qaeda and the **Taliban**, a group that provided Al Qaeda safe haven in Afghanistan.

Within months of the U.S.-led war on terrorism, the Taliban was removed from power in Afghanistan, and U.S. and UN forces occupied the country. Al Qaeda, on the other hand, still survives, though its leadership is being directly attacked and eliminated, most notably with the death of Osama bin Laden in May of 2011.

The Rise of ISIS

The rise of the Islamic State (IS, ISIL, or ISIS for short) in Iraq and Syria has led to constant instability throughout the region. The stated goal of ISIS is to revive a caliphate that unifies the entire Islamic world under ISIS's rule. The group has broadcast its terrorist methods in extremely graphic videos that feature beheadings, shootings, and other executions. This has led to universal condemnation from the international community. Similarly, the terrorist group Boko Haram (which means "Western education is forbidden") has incited conflict and violence in West African countries like Nigeria, Chad, Niger, and Cameroon. An alliance between ISIS and Boko Haram was formalized in 2015, which will only worsen the terrorist problem in the Islamic world over the coming years.

The Age of the Computer !

The single most important technological advance since the 1980s has been the rise of computers and, in turn, the Internet*.

It wasn't all that long ago when people had to use an actual atlas to plan a road trip or look up some piece of information in an encyclopedia. This is pretty hard to believe when you think about how nearly all of us carry around a tiny computer (aka your cell phone) on a daily basis, and probably can't imagine life without it.

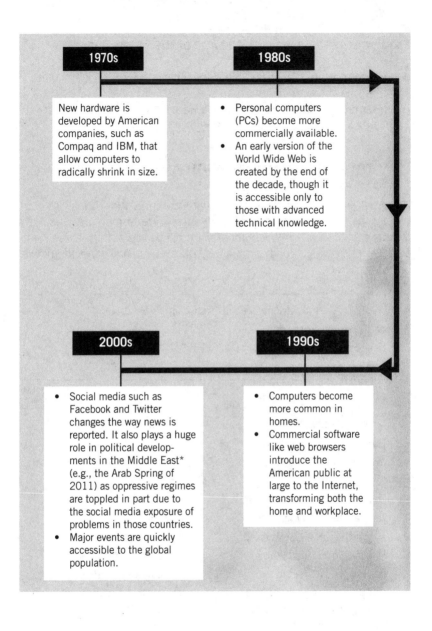

1970s

New hardware is developed by American companies, such as Compaq and IBM, that allow computers to radically shrink in size.

1980s

- Personal computers (PCs) become more commercially available.
- An early version of the World Wide Web is created by the end of the decade, though it is accessible only to those with advanced technical knowledge.

2000s

- Social media such as Facebook and Twitter changes the way news is reported. It also plays a huge role in political developments in the Middle East* (e.g., the Arab Spring of 2011) as oppressive regimes are toppled in part due to the social media exposure of problems in those countries.
- Major events are quickly accessible to the global population.

1990s

- Computers become more common in homes.
- Commercial software like web browsers introduce the American public at large to the Internet, transforming both the home and workplace.

Social media plays an enormous role in domestic politics as well. If you need an example, look no further than the 2016 presidential election and the ongoing controversy over "fake news."

c. 1900 to Present

Problems Associated with the Age of the Computer

- A growing gap in access exists between those in developed countries and those in undeveloped countries.
- Internet censorship exists in many nations, notably India and China.

Environmental Revolution

New environmental threats emerged with the Industrial Revolution, but they accelerated rapidly in the 20th century due to increased resource consumption. Current environmental problems stem from three main areas: industrialized food production, climate change, and inefficient use of resources.

Industrialized Food Production
- Large carbon footprint
- Use of pesticides (the "green revolution"*)
- Degradation of land

Climate Change	Inefficient Use of Resources
• Human activity has led to an overall increase in global temperatures. • There have been attempts to regulate carbon emissions (e.g., 1997's Kyoto Protocol). However, the United States has dragged its feet in ratifying the agreement, and Canada denounced it in 2011.	• Water, though widespread, is not a rapidly renewable resource and is often mismanaged by cities at the expense of hinterlands. • Oil is consumed at an unsustainable rate due to its use in industry and transportation.

The Green Revolution of the 20th century ushered in the use of new technologies in order to end starvation worldwide. While it is credited with feeding a billion people, there were other far-reaching effects such as reducing biodiversity and introducing harmful pesticides.

Until the 1980s, environmental solutions largely dealt with local sanitation and pollution issues. Even though the United States had created clean air and clean water legislation in the 1970s, those laws did not concern themselves with the interconnectivity of the world community. However, in recent decades, the international community has searched for solutions to these problems with a more global outlook (such as the aforementioned Kyoto Protocol). Many of these solutions have come from nongovernment actors:

Greenpeace	Green Belt Movement
• Founded in 1971 • Utilized both lobbying efforts and direct action to combat climate change, deforestation, resource degradation, and nuclear proliferation	• Created in 1977 • Based in Kenya; largely focuses on reforestation and education to promote a wider awareness of the connection between environmental issues and poverty

Earth Day
- First recognized in 1970
- Celebrated worldwide to promote environmental awareness and protection

Global Health Crises 💬

Within globalization efforts, the relief of health crises is a primary focus. Nonprofit organizations like the World Health Organization work to lower infant mortality as well as to combat various diseases, such as influenza, which kill millions in third-world countries due to a lack of appropriate medical care. Health crises in the 20th century can be seen in terms of epidemics, poverty-related diseases, and lifestyle-related diseases.

20th-Century Epidemics	Diseases Associated with Poverty	Diseases Associated with Changing Lifestyles
• Influenza • Ebola • HIV/AIDS	• Malaria • Tuberculosis • Cholera	• Obesity • Diabetes • Heart disease • Alzheimer's disease

The 20th century has also seen rapid developments in medical technologies to attack many of the diseases associated with global health crises, including the polio vaccine, antibiotics, and the artificial heart.

Changes and Continuities in the Role of Women ❶

The upheavals and changes of the 20th century resulted in dramatic changes in women's social, political, and economic roles. The global connectedness of the world made access to women's education and political freedoms far more widespread. At the same time, obstacles to female equality continued.

✛ Advancements in Women's Rights	▬ Barriers to Women's Rights
• **Suffrage** Women gained the right to vote in many parts of the world in the first part of the 20th century. By 1930, suffrage had been extended to women in much of Latin America, India, China, Japan, and most of Europe. Most of the newly independent African countries adopted women's suffrage after World War II. • **Role in Communist Revolutions** The revolutions in China and Cuba, for example, opened up educational opportunities for women, notably in medicine. • **Increased acceptance in the workplace** This was largely due to women's work in factories during the world wars when men were deployed. By the mid-1980s, women in most Westernized and industrialized countries were allowed to participate fully in the work force.	• **Asia and Africa** Women's access to formal political power remains limited in most Asian and African countries. • **Communist Party** Almost all key positions in the party were held by men. In communist China, women and female children were disproportionately impacted by the one-child policy and sterilization. • **Unequal pay** Throughout the world, women's pay has yet to fully equal that of their male counterparts. Moreover, mothers are not compensated for their role as primary caregivers of young children (the so-called "second shift" for working mothers). In agricultural economies, women's labor is under-enumerated.

Family structure changed dramatically in the 20th century, especially in the industrialized world. Birth rates dropped, birth control was widely available, and marriage rates declined as divorce and second marriages became more common.

 Ask Yourself...

1. How have some countries benefited from globalization? How have some been hurt by it?
2. In what ways are 21st-century military interventions similar to those of the 20th century? In what ways are they different?

Pulling It All Together

This chapter was packed full of information: two World Wars, the Cold War and its consequences, the end of European imperialism, the rise of the United States as a superpower, Islamic fundamentalism in the Middle East, and more. These are all huge issues, and it's difficult to work out the connections between them immediately, especially while keeping track of all the names, dates, places, and events.

To simplify things a bit, it might be helpful to look at the events of the 20th century as the result of two often-opposing forces: nationalism and globalization, themes that recur throughout the study of world history.

Nationalism

The rise of nationalism began long before the 20th century, but it certainly accelerated after 1900, giving way to fascism in countries like Germany and Italy, as well as post–World War II independence movements in India and Africa. Nationalism affected all major global events in the 20th century, particularly the World Wars and the Cold War. At times nationalism was based on broad cultural characteristics (in the case of Gandhi, for instance); at other times it was very narrowly defined, like in Nazi Germany.

Globalization

Like nationalism, the trend toward globalization started before the 20th century. Historical milestones like the Age of Exploration, the Enlightenment, and the Industrial Revolution can even be thought of as part of this shift toward globalization, as they brought people together, making the world "smaller" as a result. Due to a combination of imperialism and improvements in transportation and communication, globalization reached new heights in the 20th century into the 21st century, leading to the interconnectedness of entire economies. Today, if stock prices fall in Tokyo, for example, there is an instant impact on the U.S. market. Additionally, more and more countries have started to become culturally similar, leading many historians to argue that there is a convergence of cultures.

But a convergence of cultures has not always been embraced, particularly by countries that are trying hard to maintain strong cultural identities. As you saw in this book and as discussed above, some of the most significant events of the 20th century—and all of world history—were rooted in nationalism and the desire for self-determination.

It is this tension between nationalism and globalization that continues to chart the course of history in the modern age. Consider these themes—and the others covered in this book—as you continue to prepare for the AP World History Exam. The breadth of world history can be overwhelming, but boiling it down to a handful of themes will allow you to grasp these historical issues more easily and make connections between events. In the mean time, keep reading, keep studying, and keep thinking.

Timeline of Major Developments Since 1900 ❗

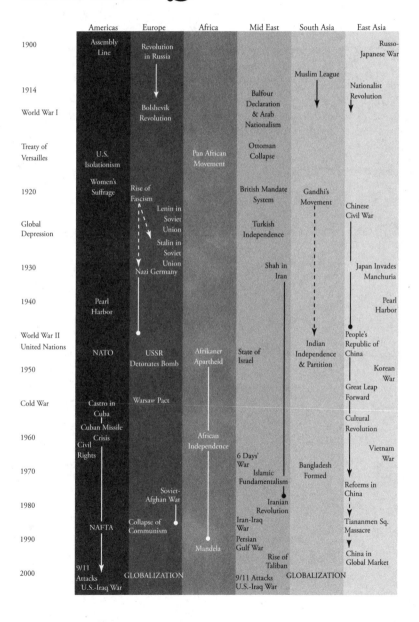

	Americas	Europe	Africa	Mid East	South Asia	East Asia
1900	Assembly Line	Revolution in Russia				Russo-Japanese War
1914				Balfour Declaration & Arab Nationalism	Muslim League	Nationalist Revolution
World War I		Bolshevik Revolution				
Treaty of Versailles	U.S. Isolationism		Pan African Movement	Ottoman Collapse		
1920	Women's Suffrage	Rise of Fascism		British Mandate System	Gandhi's Movement	Chinese Civil War
Global Depression		Lenin in Soviet Union / Stalin in Soviet Union / Nazi Germany		Turkish Independence		
1930				Shah in Iran		Japan Invades Manchuria
1940	Pearl Harbor					Pearl Harbor
World War II United Nations					Indian Independence	People's Republic of China
	NATO	USSR Detonates Bomb	Afrikaner Apartheid	State of Israel	Indian Independence & Partition	
1950						Korean War
					Great Leap Forward	
Cold War	Castro in Cuba	Warsaw Pact				Cultural Revolution
	Cuban Missile Crisis					
1960	Civil Rights		African Independence			Vietnam War
1970				6 Days' War / Islamic Fundamentalism	Bangladesh Formed	
						Reforms in China
1980		Soviet-Afghan War		Iranian Revolution		
	NAFTA	Collapse of Communism		Iran-Iraq War		Tiananmen Sq. Massacre
1990			Mandela	Persian Gulf War / Rise of Taliban		China in Global Market
2000	9/11 Attacks U.S.-Iraq War	GLOBALIZATION		9/11 Attacks U.S.-Iraq War	GLOBALIZATION	

NOTES

International Offices Listing

China (Beijing)
1501 Building A,
Disanji Creative Zone,
No.66 West Section of North 4th Ring Road Beijing
Tel: +86-10-62684481/2/3
Email: tprkor01@chol.com
Website: www.tprbeijing.com

China (Shanghai)
1010 Kaixuan Road
Building B, 5/F
Changning District, Shanghai, China 200052
Sara Beattie, Owner: Email: sbeattie@sarabeattie.com
Tel: +86-21-5108-2798
Fax: +86-21-6386-1039
Website: www.princetonreviewshanghai.com

Hong Kong
5th Floor, Yardley Commercial Building
1-6 Connaught Road West, Sheung Wan, Hong Kong
(MTR Exit C)
Sara Beattie, Owner: Email: sbeattie@sarabeattie.com
Tel: +852-2507-9380
Fax: +852-2827-4630
Website: www.princetonreviewhk.com

India (Mumbai)
Score Plus Academy
Office No.15, Fifth Floor
Manek Mahal 90
Veer Nariman Road
Next to Hotel Ambassador
Churchgate, Mumbai 400020
Maharashtra, India
Ritu Kalwani: Email: director@score-plus.com
Tel: + 91 22 22846801 / 39 / 41
Website: www.score-plus.com

India (New Delhi)
South Extension
K-16, Upper Ground Floor
South Extension Part–1,
New Delhi-110049
Aradhana Mahna: aradhana@manyagroup.com
Monisha Banerjee: monisha@manyagroup.com
Ruchi Tomar: ruchi.tomar@manyagroup.com
Rishi Josan: Rishi.josan@manyagroup.com
Vishal Goswamy: vishal.goswamy@manyagroup.com
Tel: +91-11-64501603/ 4, +91-11-65028379
Website: www.manyagroup.com

Lebanon
463 Bliss Street
AlFarra Building - 2nd floor
Ras Beirut
Beirut, Lebanon
Hassan Coudsi: Email: hassan.coudsi@review.com
Tel: +961-1-367-688
Website: www.princetonreviewlebanon.com

Korea
945-25 Young Shin Building
25 Daechi-Dong, Kangnam-gu
Seoul, Korea 135-280
Yong-Hoon Lee: Email: TPRKor01@chollian.net
In-Woo Kim: Email: iwkim@tpr.co.kr
Tel: + 82-2-554-7762
Fax: +82-2-453-9466
Website: www.tpr.co.kr

Kuwait
ScorePlus Learning Center
Salmiyah Block 3, Street 2 Building 14
Post Box: 559, Zip 1306, Safat, Kuwait
Email: infokuwait@score-plus.com
Tel: +965-25-75-48-02 / 8
Fax: +965-25-75-46-02
Website: www.scorepluseducation.com

Malaysia
Sara Beattie MDC Sdn Bhd
Suites 18E & 18F
18th Floor
Gurney Tower, Persiaran Gurney
Penang, Malaysia
Email: tprkl.my@sarabeattie.com
Sara Beattie, Owner: Email: sbeattie@sarabeattie.com
Tel: +604-2104 333
Fax: +604-2104 330
Website: www.princetonreviewKL.com

Mexico
TPR México
Guanajuato No. 242 Piso 1 Interior 1
Col. Roma Norte
México D.F., C.P.06700
registro@princetonreviewmexico.com
Tel: +52-55-5255-4495
+52-55-5255-4440
+52-55-5255-4442
Website: www.princetonreviewmexico.com

Qatar
Score Plus
Office No: 1A, Al Kuwari (Damas)
Building near Merweb Hotel, Al Saad
Post Box: 2408, Doha, Qatar
Email: infoqatar@score-plus.com
Tel: +974 44 36 8580, +974 526 5032
Fax: +974 44 13 1995
Website: www.scorepluseducation.com

Taiwan
The Princeton Review Taiwan
2F, 169 Zhong Xiao East Road, Section 4
Taipei, Taiwan 10690
Lisa Bartle (Owner): lbartle@princetonreview.com.tw
Tel: +886-2-2751-1293
Fax: +886-2-2776-3201
Website: www.PrincetonReview.com.tw

Thailand
The Princeton Review Thailand
Sathorn Nakorn Tower, 28th floor
100 North Sathorn Road
Bangkok, Thailand 10500
Thavida Bijayendrayodhin (Chairman)
Email: thavida@princetonreviewthailand.com
Mitsara Bijayendrayodhin (Managing Director)
Email: mitsara@princetonreviewthailand.com
Tel: +662-636-6770
Fax: +662-636-6776
Website: www.princetonreviewthailand.com

Turkey
Yeni Sülün Sokak No. 28
Levent, Istanbul, 34330, Turkey
Nuri Ozgur: nuri@tprturkey.com
Rona Ozgur: rona@tprturkey.com
Iren Ozgur: iren@tprturkey.com
Tel: +90-212-324-4747
Fax: +90-212-324-3347
Website: www.tprturkey.com

UAE
Emirates Score Plus
Office No: 506, Fifth Floor
Sultan Business Center
Near Lamcy Plaza, 21 Oud Metha Road
Post Box: 44098, Dubai
United Arab Emirates
Hukumat Kalwani: skoreplus@gmail.com
Ritu Kalwani: director@score-plus.com
Email: info@score-plus.com
Tel: +971-4-334-0004
Fax: +971-4-334-0222
Website: www.princetonreviewuae.com

Our International Partners

The Princeton Review also runs courses with a variety of partners in Africa, Asia, Europe, and South America.

Georgia
LEAF American-Georgian Education Center
www.leaf.ge

Mongolia
English Academy of Mongolia
www.nyescm.org

Nigeria
The Know Place
www.knowplace.com.ng

Panama
Academia Interamericana de Panama
http://aip.edu.pa/

Switzerland
Institut Le Rosey
http://www.rosey.ch/

All other inquiries, please email us at
internationalsupport@review.com